CW01333187

Air Commodore
Sir Frank Whittle

Air Commodore Sir Frank Whittle

The Man Who Invented the Turbo-jet

Robert L. Evans

AIR WORLD

First published in Great Britain in 2024 by
Air World Books
An imprint of
Pen & Sword Books Ltd
Yorkshire - Philadelphia

Copyright © Robert L. Evans

ISBN: 978 1 03611 180 9

The right of the Robert L. Evans to be identified as authors of this work has been asserted by him in accordance with the Copyright, Designs and Patents Act 1988.

A CIP catalogue record for this book is available from the British Library
All rights reserved.

No part of this book may be reproduced or transmitted in any form or by any means, electronic or mechanical including photocopying, recording or by any information storage and retrieval system, without permission from the Publisher in writing.

Typeset in INDIA by IMPEC eSolutions
Printed and bound in the England by _____

Pen & Sword Books Ltd incorporates the imprints of Pen & Sword Archaeology, Air World Books, Atlas, Aviation, Battleground, Discovery, Family History, History, Maritime, Military, Naval, Politics, Social History, Transport, True Crime, Claymore Press, Frontline Books, Praetorian Press, Seaforth Publishing and White Owl

For a complete list of Pen & Sword titles please contact:

PEN & SWORD BOOKS LTD
47 Church Street, Barnsley, South Yorkshire, S70 2AS, UK.
E-mail: enquiries@pen-and-sword.co.uk
Website: www.pen-and-sword.co.uk

or

PEN AND SWORD BOOKS,
1950 Lawrence Road, Havertown, PA 19083, USA
E-mail: Uspen-and-sword@casematepublishers.com
Website: www.penandswordbooks.com

Contents

Preface — vi

Chapter 1 Early Years — 1
Chapter 2 RAF Apprentice and Officer Cadet — 6
Chapter 3 RAF Pilot Officer — 14
Chapter 4 Back to School – RAF Henlow and Cambridge University — 29
Chapter 5 The 'Special Duty List' — 44
Chapter 6 Flight of the First Jet — 81
Chapter 7 Visit to the USA — 106
Chapter 8 Jet Engine Production Begins — 115
Chapter 9 Nationalisation — 125
Chapter 10 Post-War Developments — 137
Chapter 11 Civilian Life — 146

Postscript — 176
Appendix 1: Flight Magazine, 11 October 1945 — 179
Appendix 2: List of Patents Held by Whittle — 181
Notes — 183
Index — 187

Preface

On a beautiful day in October 1986 a Cathay Pacific Boeing 747 was just beginning its final descent into Hong Kong's Kai Tak airport. This was always a rather unnerving ending to any flight, as it required heading directly towards the spectacular skyline full of high-rise towers, before making a last-minute sharp turn towards the runway. At the controls was Captain Ian Whittle, a very experienced senior pilot who had made the landing many times. This was a rather special day, however, as sitting just behind him in the jump seat was his father, Sir Frank Whittle, himself a highly accomplished pilot and flight instructor in his youth. Captain Whittle realised that his father had not made this landing before, and might therefore be somewhat anxious at the seemingly unorthodox approach. He turned around to provide reassurance to his 79-year-old father, but soon realised that he was completely at ease, and was in fact carefully scanning the vast array of instruments in the front of the cockpit. Sir Frank was, of course, the celebrated inventor of the jet engine, and as ever was most concerned with the technical performance of the aircraft and particularly the powerful Rolls-Royce RB211 turbofan engines. As the aircraft touched down Captain Whittle was thrilled to hear his father say, 'I couldn't have done it better myself,' and later remarked that for him this was an occasion of great pride.[1]

The invention of the turbojet engine, and the determined effort to design, develop and demonstrate that such a novel new engine would replace piston engines in the air, was one of the most important technical achievements of the twentieth century. That one man accomplished this working with a small but dedicated team of engineers and craftsman in the middle of a war, and in the face of many doubters, was a truly monumental achievement. The jet engine envisaged by Frank Whittle, a young Royal Air Force cadet, truly changed aviation forever, and has had the effect of shrinking the world we live in. We think nothing today of flying between continents in a few hours, when just two or three generations ago this would have been a major expedition. In short, the jet engine, developed with great tenacity by Whittle, has made the world a village, and has introduced worldwide travel to ordinary people everywhere. This accomplishment was all the more remarkable given Whittle's humble background as the son of a highly skilled but largely uneducated mechanic and machinist. He had the necessary intellect, vision, drive and dedication, however, to make his dream of flying higher and faster a reality. This incredible accomplishment was not without considerable personal cost though, as Whittle had to face the realities of war, as well as various personal and commercial interests that nearly turned his dream into a nightmare.

My own interest in this remarkable story began on 25 May 1973, when I was near the end of my post-graduate studies in the turbomachinery laboratory of the engineering department at Cambridge University. This laboratory, dedicated to research on advanced jet engine components, had just been built and Sir Frank Whittle was invited to officially open the new facility, later to be named the Whittle Laboratory. Along with most of the other post-graduate engineering students, I hadn't really known much about the early history of my subject, and so wasn't expecting too much from the opening ceremonies. When Sir Frank arrived, with little fanfare, he was certainly polite when meeting faculty and students, but appeared to be rather diffident and reserved. This all changed, however, as he stood up without notes, and for about twenty minutes recalled some of his early struggles to design and build a completely new type of aero engine and demonstrate its ability to replace the conventional piston engines then universally used. He described, in a clear and steady voice, how the very first jet engine to run started, and then quickly accelerated to destruction even after he had closed the main fuel valve. Although he had remained at his station at the controls next to the engine, many others in attendance were not quite as calm and ran for their lives down the factory floor!

I was absolutely transfixed by the excitement that Whittle communicated, and decided that one day I would really have to learn more about this remarkable man and his incredible accomplishments. Many years later this book is the result, and I hope that the story will be as enthralling for you today as it was for me all those years ago. I would like to thank the Master and Fellows of Churchill College, Cambridge, for providing me with a visiting fellowship in order to study the extensive collection of Whittle's papers located in the college archives. I would also like to thank the Master and Fellows of Peterhouse College, Cambridge, where Whittle spent two happy years, for also providing me with a visiting fellowship and access to their collection of papers related to Whittle's time in the college. Thanks also must go to Ian Whittle, Frank's youngest son, for his encouragement in bringing this story to a wider audience, and for his insights into his father's remarkable accomplishments. And, finally, I would like to thank my wife, June, and our adult children, Katharine and Jonathan, for their constant support and encouragement that has enabled me to make this remarkable story available to a wider audience.

Chapter 1

Early Years

Frank Whittle (no other forenames) was born the first of four children to Moses and Sarah Whittle of Coventry on 1 June 1907, just three and a half years after the first powered aircraft flight by the Wright brothers. Moses Whittle and Sarah Garlick had been married in 1905 in Bolton, Lancashire, where generations of Whittles had lived and worked primarily in the cotton mills that dominated industrial activity at that time in north-west England. Both Frank's father and grandfather were named Moses, following the tradition of the Wesleyan church to name at least one son after a biblical figure. His grandfather Moses was born in 1854 in Lancashire, and was the second son of Thomas and Margaret (nee Holden) Whittle who had married in 1851. In 1875 Moses married Catherine Duckworth, and they had seven children (four boys and three girls), including Frank's father (also named Moses), who was the sixth child, born in 1882. Moses senior died in 1908, in Bolton aged just 54. When aged 11 the younger Moses had started working in a cotton mill in Bolton, where his father was employed as an 'overlooker', which corresponds to a foreman or superintendent in today's terminology. The young Moses was fascinated by the complex machinery and became a skilled mechanic working to repair looms and related machinery.

Moses and his wife Sarah went on to have three sons, Frank, Arthur and Albert, and a daughter, Catherine. By the time of Frank's birth in 1907 Moses and Sarah had moved to Coventry, then at the centre of industrial activity in Britain. Moses was then able to use his considerable practical skills as a mechanic and machinist, which he learned by working in the cotton mills further north. When Frank was born they were living in a typical terraced 'two-up and two-down' house at 72 Newcombe road in the Earlsdon district of Coventry, with a railway line at the bottom of their back garden. Young Frank started his schooling at the Earlsdon primary school at the age of 5. This was an ordinary council school, rather than one of the fee-paying prep schools that provided the usual first step on the ladder of social mobility in those days. By the time of Frank's birth the family seemed to have moved away from the church, much to the relief of Frank in later life, who seemed to find his father's name slightly embarrassing. As the oldest son, Frank had a very strong connection with his father, and always enjoyed working with him whenever possible.

Through hard work and prudent saving, by 1916 Moses was able to borrow enough capital to buy a small manufacturing company, the Leamington Valve and Piston Ring company, in Leamington Spa, just 10 miles south of Coventry. This was a good business during the years of the First World War, and was aimed at serving the growing number of vehicle repair shops. The business prospered and the young Whittle family moved to Leamington Spa, where Frank's mother enrolled him at a small fee-paying primary school. Frank felt very uncomfortable in this environment, however, and after just one day his mother relented and he transferred to the nearby Milverton primary school. This was opened in 1887 as a boys' school and is still in use today. He prospered at Milverton, and after several years there his outstanding ability in mathematics and science enabled him to win a scholarship to nearby Leamington College for Boys. This school was founded in 1844 as the Warwickshire Proprietary College with the aim of providing 'for the sons of the nobility, clergy and gentry, a sound classical and mathematical education in accordance with the principles of the established church'.[2] The school struggled with financial difficulties for some time, and in 1851 it became a fee-paying public school, catering to the sons of local landowners and members of the growing middle class. In 1855, however, in an enlightened move, the college rules were amended to allow the sons of tradesmen to be admitted for the first time. By the time Whittle joined the school it had become very much a minor public school, but still had a strong commitment to solid teaching for the mix of middle-class and working-class pupils.

The move to Leamington College proved to be very beneficial for young Frank, and he thrived on the emphasis placed on the fundamentals of mathematics, physics and chemistry. He was, however, a small boy of slight build and did not enjoy the usual sporting activities at school. He spent most of his spare time either in the school library, or the nearby Leamington public library scouring books on popular science and any more technical volumes he could find. One of these, for example, was a book by the Slovak engineer and physicist Aurel Stodola[3] on the theory of steam turbines, then a relatively new technology. Although Whittle wasn't able at that time to absorb all of the theory, he did use much of the knowledge he gained later on while working with the British Thomson Houston Company to produce his own design of gas turbine blading. At the same time Frank was already helping his father after school and enjoyed learning how to use a wide range of hand tools and the small collection of machine tools in his father's automotive repair shop. As a result he became quite a proficient machinist at a very early age. The combination of practical hands-on machine shop experience and theoretical understanding obtained from textbooks would provide the foundation for Frank's approach later in life to solving complex engineering problems.

As with many young boys at that time, Whittle was fascinated with aeroplanes, which had first flown only a few years before. Whenever an aeroplane flew overhead at the time there would be great excitement, bringing small boys out of their houses to gaze into the sky in wonderment. The start of the First World War in 1914 resulted in the production of a wide range of small, lightweight aeroplanes, which were used for reconnaissance purposes and also as fighter aircraft and light bombers. These were mainly biplanes, constructed largely of hardwood frames covered in canvas and powered by a range of relatively small air-cooled engines driving a single propeller. There were more than thirty different types ultimately used by the allies during the conflict, including famous marques such as the Avro 504, the Sopwith Camel and a wide range of both single and dual-seat aircraft manufactured by the De Havilland Aircraft Company, the Royal Aircraft factory and others. These were flown by pilots of the Royal Flying Corps, which had been formed in 1912, and the Royal Naval Air Service until early 1918, when these two services were merged to form the new Royal Air Force. The biplanes, of course, were very rudimentary compared to the aircraft of today. They represented the very latest in the technology of the time, however, and young Frank Whittle was mesmerised by them. He soon started to build model aeroplanes, and with the skills he had developed in his father's workshop he quickly became very proficient at building accurate replicas of the wondrous machines he saw overhead.

After the war ended in 1918, Moses Whittle's business, along with many others, experienced a severe downturn. With money being in short supply at home, Frank began to realise he would need to find secure work after leaving Leamington College. With stories of the heroic role that flyers had played in the war fresh in their minds, it was natural that many young boys would dream of becoming pilots in the fledgling Royal Air Force. Pilots were commissioned officers, however, and were normally selected from the prestigious public schools catering to upper- and middle-class students. This was therefore not a route open to Whittle, but with his increasing interest in model aeroplanes, and considerable practical skills, he decided that he should join the RAF to train as an aeroplane mechanic. After completing the first term of the sixth form at Leamington College, Whittle applied in 1922 at the age of 15 to become an aircraft mechanic apprentice at RAF Halton near Wendover in Hampshire. This was one of the largest bases of the fledgling RAF at the time, and the Royal Flying Corps had moved its aircraft mechanics training school from Farnborough to Halton in 1916. From 1917 on the school was well equipped with new workshops, primarily built by German prisoners of war, and became the RAF's No.1 School of Technical Training.

Whittle had passed the written entrance exam easily, but was distraught to learn that he had failed the mandatory physical exam. At age 15 he was a slight boy just over 5ft tall, which prevented him from passing the tests of fitness and strength deemed necessary for the potential heavy lifting required of an aircraft mechanic. Although he was bitterly disappointed by this setback, Whittle showed some of the early determination that was a hallmark of his later career by embarking on a regimen of high-protein diet and bodybuilding while completing the second term of his sixth form studies at Leamington College. His dedication to improving his physique and fitness during his final school term enabled him to pass the RAF physical fitness examination some six months later when he applied again for an apprenticeship. As a precaution against encountering the same examiners, however, this time he applied to RAF Cranwell. The well-known officer training college was also the home of an aircraft mechanics apprenticeship school to serve the rapidly increasing need for skilled mechanics that could not be accommodated at RAF Halton. Whittle, who would ultimately obtain the rank of air commodore, started his RAF career as a 16-year-old 'boy apprentice' in early October 1923.

Chapter 2

RAF Apprentice and Officer Cadet

Whittle began his air mechanic (or 'fitter', which they were called at the time) apprenticeship with great enthusiasm. He was thrilled to be on the impressive Cranwell station primarily used to train officer cadets and which included a flying training school. Initially he also harboured a secret hope that he may be one step closer to fulfilling his lifelong ambition of learning to fly. The air mechanic apprenticeship was a three-year course aimed at providing a thorough practical understanding of all aircraft structural components as well as a detailed knowledge of the different types of aircraft engines then in use. The days would be filled with a combination of classroom lessons and practical exercises in the extensive workshops. Whittle also had much more practical experience than most of his peers as a result of his extensive experience from a young age working in his father's machine shop. He was a diligent apprentice, and happily threw himself into every aspect of the rigorous training provided, while at the same time keeping an eye on the officer cadets learning to fly whenever he could. He did find, however, that the very rudimentary skills being taught in the first year, such as the use of hand tools, were of little benefit to someone who already had well-developed skills in this area.

One aspect of RAF life that did not appeal to Whittle was the strict discipline required for the routine 'square bashing' exercises that were (and still are) common to all of the armed forces. Whittle had always been something of a free spirit who liked to think for himself, and resented being required to take part in the frequent parade exercises and robust physical training that are the hallmark of military training everywhere. On balance, however, he believed that the privilege of being able to work with aircraft outweighed having to spend so much time on seemingly unrelated activities. He also felt privileged to be able to watch new pilots being trained, and never gave up the feeling that what he really wanted to do was to fly himself. He soon realised, though, that as an apprentice aircraft mechanic this was highly unlikely to be a realistic career objective. There was one thing that singled Whittle out from most of his contemporary apprentices, however, and that was his involvement in the model aeroplane club. While most apprentices found that involvement in the club could provide some welcome distraction from the rigid discipline of their training, Whittle took it far more seriously. By this time he already understood the theory of flight better than most, partly due to spending an extra term in the sixth form at Leamington College after his initial failure of the physical fitness tests at Halton. In large measure, however, it was due to his ability to quickly grasp the mathematical and physical concepts that were essential to understanding aerodynamics and the theory of flight and then to apply these to his model aircraft designs.

Whittle as Air Mechanic Apprentice

As a result of his natural abilities and inclination to 'take charge' when he knew more than those around him, Whittle quickly became the leader of the model aircraft club at Cranwell, and spent most of his spare time designing and building new models. His most ambitious project was a model with a wingspan of over 10ft, powered by a 2-stroke engine selected because of its high power-to-weight ratio. This model flew successfully, and became quite a showpiece for the model aircraft club, drawing the attention not only of the apprenticeship instructors, but also the Cranwell commanding officer (or CO), Group Captain Robert Borton. Borton was so impressed with the activities of the model aeroplane club that whenever he toured visitors around the station he invariably took them to watch its activities, and Whittle was usually asked to demonstrate one of the models that were largely his creation. As a result, the CO became familiar with young Whittle and realised that he was a cut above most of the apprentices, both in his knowledge of aircraft fundamentals and his abilities as a first-class mechanic.

With a class of some 600 apprentices, it was a very happy result for Whittle that he would come to be noticed by the busy CO, who was responsible not only for the apprenticeship course but also for the officer cadet trainees. Towards the end of his apprenticeship Whittle was also detailed to act as an orderly to the CO. This required him to accompany him on his daily rounds of the base, and of course this enabled the CO to learn more about the suitability of young Whittle as a possible officer cadet candidate.[4] At the time, of course, Whittle didn't really think much about this, as he was just keen to demonstrate his knowledge of aircraft generally, but he later realised that the commandant had taken note of the unusual abilities of this young apprentice.

At the end of the three-year apprenticeship course there were a series of comprehensive examinations, and as in most public schools at that time the candidates were ranked in order of their accomplishments. Whittle ended up ranked as sixth out of the entire group of 600 apprentices, based on his exam results. However, he also had the advantage of having caught the eye of the CO through his outstanding performance with the model aeroplane club. Whittle's position as the CO's orderly also enabled the commandant to judge whether or not he could be a potential officer candidate. A tradition had also developed in which the five top-ranked candidates from the apprenticeship course would be put forward for officer cadetships. Whittle was very disappointed, of course, to learn that he had just missed out on being selected for a cadetship, and reconciled himself to a life as an air mechanic, perhaps ending up as a senior non-commissioned officer. When the first five candidates were duly sent for the stiff physical examinations required for entry to the officer cadet wing of the college, Whittle was told to go with them. In what he later realised was probably one of those life-changing experiences, it turned out that one of the top five candidates failed the physical examination, and Whittle was duly elevated to become an officer cadet candidate. The irony was not lost on him that this was the second time in his young life that a tough physical screening regime had helped to support his ambition to fly.

Then, following a brief holiday, Whittle returned to RAF Cranwell as an officer cadet. The next two years of his cadetship, which included flying training, was one of the happiest periods of his life and enabled him to demonstrate his unique talent and abilities to the full. Most of his fellow officer cadets were from middle-class families and had attended the more traditional public schools, as most private schools were then labelled. Most of the cadets were younger than Whittle as they had come straight from school to Cranwell as officer cadets. They also did not have the thorough practical mechanical training and understanding of flight mechanics that Whittle had gained as an apprentice mechanic and leader of the model aeroplane club. Whittle turned out to be a 'natural' pilot, and quickly showed that he not only had a thorough understanding of the theory of flight, but could put this knowledge to very practical use by demonstrating that he could fly at the very limits of the aeroplane's capabilities. It also helped that Whittle was quite fearless, and while this sometimes resulted in remonstrations from his flight instructors it also singled him out as someone who should be encouraged to take on some of the more demanding flying assignments in the fledgling RAF.

As part of the programme of studies as an officer cadet at Cranwell every student had to submit a short thesis at the end of each term on a subject of interest to them and relevant to the RAF. Near the end of his studies as a cadet in 1928 Whittle submitted a thesis entitled 'Future Developments in Aircraft Design'. This remarkable forty-nine-page handwritten document included calculations and sketches describing the mechanical and thermodynamic design of his novel engine concept. In this very detailed thesis Whittle first outlined the challenges of building aeroplanes capable of flying much higher and faster than was possible at the time. He recognised that this would be necessary if long-distance travel by air was ever to be feasible, and that currently available aeroplane designs, and especially their engines, were not suitable for this type of flying. He began by describing the challenges of developing power from piston engines at high altitude where the air density was much lower than near the ground, thus severely limiting the ability of air-breathing engines to develop sufficient power. He then went on to discuss the possibility of using a propulsion system that was completely different from anything else then known. The thesis described in detail both the thermodynamic and mechanical design of a completely novel form of propulsion system. This new and innovative engine design would replace the conventional piston engine with a system designed to provide a jet of hot exhaust gases. These gases would then be used to drive a turbine connected to a conventional propeller. This was the kernel of what came to be known as 'turboprop' engines, which are still widely used today, primarily in smaller passenger aircraft and large military transport planes. This development also led ultimately to commercial development of the turbojet engine envisaged by Whittle after leaving Cranwell. These engines are now universally used in commercial airliners that we take for granted today.

The brief introductory paragraph of Whittle's thesis, reproduced below, shows the remarkable insight that he already had about the future of powered flight:

The flight of the aeroplane 'Southern Cross' from San Francisco to Sydney via Honolulu and Suva marks the latest step in aircraft performance, yet it is less than a score of years since the crossing of the channel by Bleriot was acclaimed as a marvellous feat. The development of aircraft has made some astounding strides, and it is reasonable to suppose that this development is going to continue. It is a hazardous business to forecast the future, especially in these days of discovery, where science may at any moment make revolutionary discoveries. There are three ways of speculating on the future. There is the immediate future, the further future, and the far future. The object of this work is to discuss the 'middle' future, with a certain amount of speculation which probably overlaps the immediate future.

Development will take place along the following lines.

1) Increase in range
2) Increase of speed
3) Increase of reliability
4) Decrease of structural weight
5) More economical flight
6) Increase of ceiling
7) Increase of load carrying capacity
8) Greater ability to withstand the elements

Many of these will be interdependent, for instance a decrease in structural weight will result in increased range, etc.

With the benefit of hindsight, of course, it can be seen that all of the advantages claimed by Whittle for jet propulsion in his thesis have been demonstrated very clearly. In the remaining part of the introduction to his thesis Whittle describes some of the advantages of turbines, which by then were primarily designed to generate electricity using high-pressure steam as the energy source. He hinted at the possible use of turbines for aircraft propulsion by saying:

> It seems that as the turbine is the most efficient prime mover known, it is possible that it will be developed for aircraft especially if some means of driving a turbine by petrol could be devised. A steam turbine is quite impractical owing to the weight of boilers, condensers, etc. A petrol-driven turbine would be more efficient than a steam turbine as there need be no loss of heat through the flues, all the exhaust going through the nozzles.

He went on to describe the thermodynamic cycle of a unique engine designed to replace the conventional petrol-fuelled piston engine, which was then universally used to drive the propellers of all aircraft. At this stage Whittle envisaged the use of a petrol-fuelled piston engine to drive a conventional reciprocating compressor. The compressed air and hot exhaust gases would then be mixed and used to drive a turbine wheel connected to a conventional propeller. A drawing of this proposed design based on the hand-drawn sketch from his thesis is shown in Plate 5. It can be seen that the central cylinder is a conventional petrol-fuelled piston engine that drives the two outer cylinders used to compress air. The compressed air, as well as the high-pressure exhaust gases from the engine cylinder are then used to drive a turbine wheel connected directly to a conventional propeller. It was some time after writing his thesis that Whittle realised the potential for a pure jet of hot exhaust gases from the turbine to produce all the thrust required for high-speed flight. This would then become the basis of all his future developments of the new 'jet engine'.

Although Whittle did not feel at ease with most of his younger and predominantly public school-educated fellow cadets, he did get along well with Rolf Dudley-Williams, who shared a hut with him during this period at Cranwell. Williams was from a modest family in Plymouth, where his father was a master draper. He had come to Cranwell as an officer cadet after completing his schooling at Plymouth College. The two young cadets got on well and became close friends during their two years at Cranwell. As Whittle developed his initial ideas for jet propulsion he would often use Williams as a sounding board by describing his futuristic plans in some detail. Following his graduation from Cranwell and serving as a pilot officer, Williams would go on to a business career after being invalided out of the RAF following a flying accident. He kept in touch with Whittle, however, and with his business connections he would be instrumental in helping him secure initial funding for his turbojet project. Williams ultimately became managing director of Power Jets, the company established to further Whittle's dream of building a working jet engine. After the war, when Power Jets was finally wound up, Williams became a Conservative politician, serving as the MP for Exeter from 1951 to 1968. He was appointed as the Parliamentary Private Secretary (PPS) to the Secretary of State for War in 1958, and then served in the same role for the Minister of Agriculture from 1961 to 1964. In 1964 he was created a Baronet (a hereditary form of Knighthood), and then changed his surname by deed poll to Dudley-Williams by combining his middle name and original surname. After his death in 1987 at the age of 79 he was succeeded in the baronetcy by his son, Sir Alastair Dudley-Williams.

Chapter 3

RAF Pilot Officer

Whittle graduated second in his class and was commissioned as a pilot officer at the age of 21 on 28 July 1928. He also won the Andy Fellowes Memorial Prize for Aeronautical Sciences for his thesis and was commended for being an 'above average to exceptional' pilot.[5] At the same time his instructors had commented that he had a tendency towards showing off that sometimes resulted in dangerous low flying.

After graduation from Cranwell, Whittle was posted to 111 Squadron at RAF Hornchurch, east of London in Essex. This station, originally built to defend London during the First World War, had just been reopened to house the unit, which was equipped with Armstrong Whitworth Siskin III fighters. The Siskin III was a well-regarded and highly manoeuvrable biplane, and one of the first combat aircraft to use a supercharged engine in order to provide much better performance at high altitude. The station commander at the time was Keith Park, a New Zealander who would go on to become a celebrated RAF commander during the Battle of Britain in the Second World War, ultimately retiring as an air chief marshal. At Hornchurch Whittle quickly demonstrated his highly developed skills as a pilot and he also gained a reputation for being completely fearless. These attributes sometimes resulted in him being admonished by his superiors for carrying out demonstrations of aerobatics and low flying near heavily populated areas. Within a year, however, these very skills led to him being sent in late 1929 to train as a flying instructor at the Central Flying School at RAF Wittering, near Stamford in Lincolnshire.

As a gifted pilot, and with his complete understanding of the theory of flight and the technical abilities of an aeroplane, Whittle developed into a highly regarded instructor at Wittering. During his spare time he continued to work on his ideas for jet propulsion and to share these with anyone who would listen. One of the instructors at the Central Flying School was W.E.P. (Pat) Johnson, also known by his friends in the RAF as 'Johnny'. In civilian life Johnson had trained as a patent examiner, and after listening to Whittle's proposals he could immediately see the potential benefits of his ideas. He encouraged Whittle to continue developing his concept, and to show his ideas to the station commandant. After explaining his concept to the commandant, a meeting was arranged with Dr A.A. Griffith, who was working on related gas turbine propulsion ideas at the Royal Aircraft Establishment (RAE). The gas turbine engine, consisting of an air compressor, combustor and turbine, was a known concept, but had not yet been commercialised, in part due to the lack of suitable materials to withstand the high continuous temperatures required. Griffith was one of the few people who understood the potential benefits of using a lightweight gas turbine engine, but assumed it would be used to provide shaft power to drive a conventional propeller. In what later became the 'turboprop' design, the turbine is sized to provide sufficient power to drive both the compressor and a propeller. In Whittle's new concept, however, the turbine was sized to be just powerful enough to drive the compressor while the remaining energy in the exhaust gases would be used directly to generate a high-speed propulsion jet. Griffith indicated that he did not think the propelling jet concept would be as efficient as a conventional propeller design, and as a result Whittle's turbojet idea was deemed to be of no interest to the Air Ministry.

With hindsight it is intriguing to speculate on the official rejection of the turbojet concept as proposed by Whittle. Griffith had been working almost single-handedly on gas turbine research since 1926 with little official recognition of his efforts. The concept of a gas turbine had been well known since its invention by John Barber in 1791,[6] although he was unsuccessful in building a successful engine. This was due in large part to the poor efficiency of the compressor and turbine and the need for sustained high temperatures. Conventional wisdom, even at the time that Griffith was working on the concept, was that there were no available materials that could withstand the sustained high temperatures required. Of course, Griffith's rejection of Whittle's ideas could also perhaps be a case of the 'not-invented-here' syndrome that can often make it difficult for lone inventors to obtain support for their ideas. Or, it could just be that Griffith did not think that the turbojet concept would be suitable for the relatively slow-speed aeroplanes then in production. As it turns out, today the turbojet and turbofan concepts, both of which were foreseen by Whittle, are universally used for high-speed aircraft flying near to, and above, the speed of sound, while turboprop engines are used for slower-speed and shorter flight applications.

The official rejection of his ideas was a blow to Whittle, but he was not one to give up easily and vowed to continue on in his spare time. Although the Air Ministry was not interested in Whittle's ideas, Johnson continued to believe they were very promising and encouraged Whittle to patent his concept for jet propulsion. He helped Whittle prepare a patent application, which was duly submitted to the patent office on 16 January 1930. The patent, entitled 'Improvements relating to the Propulsion of Aircraft and other Vehicles', was finally published as 'Complete Accepted' on 16 April 1931.[7] As a serving officer, any intellectual property developed by Whittle was automatically the property of the government. However, following Griffith's rejection of the turbojet concept, Whittle was able to get official permission from the Air Ministry to personally pursue his turbojet concept on his own time. An agreement between the President of the Air Council, the legal representative of the RAF, and Whittle was duly obtained on 3 October 1930. This agreement stated that 'the invention shall be the absolute property of the inventor and may be dealt with and disposed of by him as he shall think fit'. There was some official 'hedging of bets', however, as the agreement went on to say, 'but, such disposition shall be subject to modifications and provisions as the President may require'.[8]

The patent, by today's standards is deceptively brief, consisting of just three pages of text and two figures. The concept is described succinctly however, and shows the clear and concise thinking that was the hallmark of Whittle's career. The thermodynamic basis of jet propulsion can be very simply described using the pressure-volume diagram shown in Figure 1 of the patent. This figure is now contained in most introductory engineering thermodynamics textbooks for mechanical engineering students, and is the starting point used to design any turbojet engine. The simple description of Figure 1 (see Plate 6), taken from the patent, clearly describes the complete thermodynamic cycle of a turbojet engine. The thermal cycle employed, which is shown in Fig.1, is a pressure volume diagram in which:

> AG represents the atmospheric line.
> DC represents compression.
> CE represents heating at constant pressure.
> EF represents the portion of expansion that is utilised to do the work of compression.
> FG represents the expansion to the atmosphere providing thrust by fluid reaction.

The key to Whittle's invention of the turbojet is the last line, describing the expansion, FG, of the combustion gases leaving the turbine nozzles to atmospheric pressure. This expansion results in acceleration of the exhaust gases from the engine, producing the jet reaction thrust that drives the aeroplane forward. This brilliantly simple description provides the fundamental thermodynamic basis of all turbojets from the original Whittle experimental engine to today's aircraft engines. As a slight caveat to that statement, the technically astute reader will forgive the author for ignoring the fact that most modern jet engines are actually turbofan engines that include a very large fan, or propeller, at the front of the engine. In this way, modern turbofan engines, which can provide up to 100,000lb of thrust, are really a combination of turbojet and turboprop engines. The turbofan engine was also conceived early on by Whittle, who often described it as the next step in jet propulsion development. Johnson became one of Whittle's close collaborators on jet engine design and continued to act as his patent agent during the subsequent development of the engine.

Figure 2 from the patent (see Plate 7) shows the mechanical arrangement of the turbojet engine envisioned by Whittle. The left-hand side of the figure shows the compressor casing 1, components 2 to 5, which illustrate an axial-flow compressor stage, and finally 7 and 8, which relate to the radial blading and diffuser section of a centrifugal compressor. The compressed air that is then gathered in the header 9 is fed into one or more combustion chambers, shown as component 10. Fuel is then admitted through a series of nozzles, 11, where it is ignited so that the hot exhaust gases collected in the header 12 are fed through an axial-flow turbine stage depicted by the turbine rotor, 13, the turbine rotor blades or 'buckets', 14, and stator blades, 15. Component 16 depicts the rotor shaft, or 'spindle' as Whittle calls it, which joins the compressor to the turbine. Finally, the combustion products pass through a series of convergent-divergent nozzles, 17, which are used to expand the exhaust gases to a high velocity. It is this final component, which uses one or more nozzles to accelerate the exhaust gas in order to directly provide jet thrust, which provides the key claim in this patent.

The basic gas turbine, as patented by John Barber in 1791, was designed to provide pure rotary shaft power. No one before Whittle, however, had ever suggested using the hot exhaust gases exiting from the turbine to provide thrust directly through jet reaction. This was the defining genius of Whittle's discovery, and turned out to be the future of aircraft propulsion. It is also very interesting to see that Whittle's original patent envisaged the use of both an axial-flow compressor and a centrifugal compressor working in series. During subsequent development of the engine, in the interests of simplicity, he insisted on using just a single centrifugal compressor stage when others were suggesting that an axial-flow design would be more efficient. Many years later, and after much development work, the axial-flow compressor has become highly efficient and is now used as the 'standard' design for all but the smallest turbojet or turboprop engines.

Following publication of the patent, Whittle made enquiries with a number of aircraft firms to see if any of them would be interested in his novel new propulsion system. Perhaps not surprisingly, none of the companies he contacted showed an interest in working with this young RAF officer to develop what must have seemed to them to be a radical and wholly untried concept for aircraft propulsion. He had also written to a number of academics who he knew had been working on gas turbine concepts. A typical answer came from Mr W.J. Kearton, a lecturer at the University of Liverpool, who said that 'gas turbines are fine in theory, but very difficult in practice'. As a result of his enquiries, Whittle came to the conclusion that with little industrial interest in his concept, he would have to take it on himself. Of course, this would not be easy to do, given that he still had a full-time job as an RAF officer, and no financial means to pursue his dream.

The year 1930 turned out to be an eventful and busy time for Whittle. In addition to his training as a flight instructor and his work with Johnson on patenting his jet propulsion concept, his personal life was also becoming more complex. During his time at Cranwell Whittle would often travel back home to Rugby during leave periods to spend time with his family. On one of these visits he met Dorothy Lee, the daughter of Edgar and Margaret Lee, who lived near his parents' house in Rugby. Dorothy was some three years older than Frank, but as a first-born son and RAF cadet Frank was quite a mature young man, and they began dating from the time he turned 18. They continued a somewhat on and off again relationship while Whittle was away and very busy with his training. However, once Whittle had established his full-time career in the RAF the couple decided it was time to take the next step in their relationship. He proposed to Dorothy, and they were married on 24 May 1930. The marriage was somewhat controversial at the time, since the RAF's usual guideline was that an officer should not be married before the age of 30, and that no 'marriage allowance' would be paid to officers marrying before that age. The wedding took place in Mary's home town of Coventry, but Whittle's parents did not attend as they evidently felt that marriage at such an early age (Whittle was just about to turn 23) would compromise what was a promising RAF career. There was also some feeling that young Frank was marrying 'above his station', as Dorothy's family were decidedly middle class. Frank and Dorothy would go on to have two sons, Francis David (known as David), born in 1931, and Ian Lee, born in 1934. David had meningitis as a child, and although he was accomplished academically, he was socially quite awkward and became a rather reclusive individual. He attended lectures at St Andrew's University but had little contact with his family, dying in 2013 without marrying or having children of his own. Ian would eventually follow in his father's footsteps, joining the RAF and training as a pilot. After leaving the RAF, Ian would continue his flying career as a commercial airline pilot. He ended his career as a senior captain flying Boeing 747s for Cathay Pacific Airways.

Towards the end of 1930, and with his patent work with Johnson complete, Whittle made a connection that would turn out to be very important for the future of the jet engine. This was initiated by Johnson, whose brother was a housemaster at Rugby School, and had some connections with the large industrial company British Thomson Houston Co. (BTH), a major employer in Rugby.[9] BTH began as a subsidiary of the American Thomson-Houston company, which had merged with the Edison General Electric company begun by Thomas Edison to form the General Electric Company in the 1890s. BTH's major business was as designers and manufacturers of large equipment for electricity generation. Crucially, this included steam turbines, which were (and still are) widely used to power large electrical generators in power stations. Johnson persuaded his brother to introduce Whittle to Frederick Samuelson, who was the chief turbine engineer at BTH. Johnson reasoned that a turbine is a turbine, after all, and it should not be very much of a stretch for a large manufacturer of steam turbines to turn their hand to what was essentially a gas turbine design. Although the BTH engineers were quite interested in Whittle's proposal, they weren't able to convince senior managers, who were very doubtful that there was any kind of a future for gas turbines, let alone a jet propulsion engine. They also felt that it was not something they could get involved in with their own limited funds during the height of the economic recession, but agreed to keep in touch with Whittle should he be successful in obtaining funding for his proposal. They parted on amiable terms and Whittle agreed to keep in touch. He ended up making several visits to the BTH factory during visits back to nearby Coventry, where his wife's parents still lived.

Following completion of his flying instructor course at Wittering, Whittle was posted to No. 2 Flying Training School at RAF

Digby in late 1930 as an instructor. Digby airfield, near the village of Scopwick in Lincolnshire, had been used since 1917 for pilot training. Before the formation of the RAF in 1918 it was used to train the first group of naval aviators attached to the Royal Navy. By the time Whittle arrived in 1930 it had become one of the main pilot training facilities for the RAF, with a number of famous commanders, including 'Bomber Harris' and Arthur Tedder, who would go on to become Lord Tedder and Marshal of the Royal Air Force later in the Second World War. Whittle found his instructor duties to be more challenging and enjoyable than he had imagined, but he was still spending much of his spare time working on his jet propulsion concepts. At Digby the Avro 504N was used for training new pilots. The Avro 504 had been built in very large numbers since 1913 and were the most widely used British fighter during the First World War. By the time Whittle started flying them in 1930 they were no longer considered as front-line fighters but were widely used for instruction purposes.

During this time Whittle was also detailed to take part in the annual air show at RAF Hendon. Whittle's part in this was described as 'crazy flying', which consisted of a series of aerobatic manoeuvres in tandem with another pilot. Whittle and his partner planned a series of stunts, including mock near-collisions and 'hopping' manoeuvres that were very hard on the somewhat delicate undercarriage of the Avro 504. This was to be quite a spectacular display, in which two aircraft would also fly erratically across the airfield, carefully avoiding each other as they passed very closely. Unfortunately, during rehearsals for the event at RAF Digby, Whittle collided with his opposite number in one of these close encounters, resulting in the writing off of both aeroplanes! Due to the relatively slow speeds and low altitude involved it was fortunate that both pilots escaped unscathed. They did not impress their flight commander, however, who came over to Whittle and said, 'Why don't you take all my bloody aeroplanes into the middle of the aerodrome and set fire to them – it's quicker.'[10] The actual performance at Hendon was conducted without mishap, however, and met with great appreciation from the large crowd in attendance. This marked the end of Whittle's crazy flying days, and his exceptional flying skills were put to use in more pragmatic ways.

By the end of 1930, with Dorothy expecting their first child, and with suitable family housing in the Digby area hard to find, Whittle felt that a change of scenery would be welcome. Although he had enjoyed his time as an instructor, it was becoming quite routine for him and he thought that a more challenging assignment, perhaps with modern aircraft, would be more interesting. He therefore asked his commanding officer for a 'posting', and in early 1931 he was assigned to the Marine Aircraft Experimental Establishment at Felixstowe as a floatplane test pilot. Upon the formation of the RAF in 1918 the Felixstowe station was called the Seaplane Experimental Station, Felixstowe, but at the end of the First World War it was closed. It was then reopened and named the Marine Aircraft Experimental Establishment in 1924 until the end of the Second World War.

Initially, Whittle was involved in testing seaplanes that were launched and recovered from the beach. As the weather was usually quite rough, the amount of flying time was rather limited, which Whittle found to be not to his liking. He was also assigned to one task, however, which he found almost too exciting, especially as at this time he could not swim and had never been to sea before. This was a 'ditching test', in which he was asked to simulate an emergency situation by deliberating crashing the seaplane into the sea from a height of about 2m. When he did this Whittle was quite alarmed when the cockpit quickly filled with water, and then the fuselage tipped into a vertical position before coming back down to a more normal horizontal position. He was wearing a lifejacket, of course, and was able to calmly remove the inflatable dinghy stored in the back of the aeroplane and make his way back to the ship, much to the relief of the assembled ship's company, which had been watching nervously. There is a very nice photograph reproduced in *Jet* (Plate 8 below) in which Whittle is paddling calmly back to the ship while the biplane is sinking just behind him.

During Whittle's time at Felixstowe he also took part in tests of catapult launching of seaplanes from the decks of conventional warships. At the time there was considerable interest in the use of aircraft launched from such ships as a possible forward reconnaissance tool. It was thought that the successful deployment of a small aeroplane from a cruiser or destroyer could alleviate the need for much larger and more expensive aircraft carriers used in a reconnaissance role. This was really a forerunner of today's practice of carrying a helicopter on board many conventional warships in order to conduct forward reconnaissance operations. As usual, Whittle committed himself completely to this new assignment, and made a valuable contribution to the understanding of catapult launches from warships without regard for the considerable personal risks involved. These trials were conducted from the deck of HMS *Ark Royal*, which was built in 1914 and was the first ship to transport seaplanes. Following the end of the First World War, *Ark Royal* was put in reserve, but was then re-commissioned in 1930 to evaluate the catapult launching of seaplanes. She was the forerunner of several more modern aircraft carriers of the same name. Altogether, Whittle performed forty-seven catapult launches, sometimes up to nine in one day.

While working at Felixstowe, Whittle also experienced one of the most alarming, and in retrospect amusing, incidents in his long RAF career. The seaplanes being used were two-seat Fairey IIIF biplanes, and the catapult testing often included an observer in the rear cockpit seat. On one such occasion Whittle was accompanied by Flight Lieutenant Kirk as the observer in the rear seat. Immediately after launch, Whittle felt the tail of the plane drop unexpectedly, and he struggled to reach level flight. He took a quick look back at the rear of the airplane, and was alarmed to see that Kirk was out of the cockpit, and sitting on the rear tailplane with one hand holding on to the tailfin bracing wire! He had failed to fasten his seatbelt, and had then lost his grip on the cockpit coaming during the rapid acceleration on the catapult, resulting in his slipping completely out of the cockpit. Nevertheless, Kirk seemed quite nonchalant, and gave Whittle a 'thumbs up' to indicate he was safe. With great skill Whittle then proceeded to make an emergency landing. This was much more difficult than a normal landing, since he had to maintain a higher than usual landing speed in order to keep the airplane level with the additional weight at the back. Whittle accomplished this, however, and Kirk managed to clamber back into the cockpit. Once back on board the ship both he and Kirk were given a rousing welcome by the very relieved captain and crew! Although his exceptional flying feat was widely acclaimed, Whittle was actually given a mild official rebuke since it was his responsibility to ensure that Kirk had his seatbelt fastened.

Whittle then wrote to the Commanding Office of HMS *Ark Royal* in a rather understated way, as follows:

Sir,

I have the honour to submit this my report on an incident which occurred during catapult trials on Monday, 4th July, 1932. I was pilot carrying out test No. 1, comprising a series of launches at reduced wind speeds. For the 3rd, 4th, 5th and 6th launches I was flying III.F. S.1800. I carried one passenger for each of these four launches.

Immediately after the 6th launch, which was carried out at no wind speed, and with Flight Lieutenant Kirk as passenger,

I felt the aircraft suddenly become very tail heavy, and the nose started to rise rapidly. As the speed was very low, about 55 knots, this was very alarming, and I at first thought that the tail plane was badly damaged. I succeeded in getting the aircraft on to a more or less even keel by pushing the control column hard forward. I then turned to look at the tail plane and saw a figure on the tail plane which I at first thought was an airman who had somehow failed to get clear. A second glance showed me that it was my passenger, Flt. Lieutenant Kirk, who had now struggled into a sitting position and was clinging to the tail plane. He signalled that he was safe (thumbs up). I succeeded in landing the aircraft safely by flying on to the water with half engine.

As usual, Whittle did not confine himself only to the flying duties assigned to him, but continued to explore the more technical aspects of his work on his own time. He thought that the catapult design on *Ark Royal* was rather primitive, and could likely be improved. This resulted in a technical paper, 'Description of a Proposed Catapult Principle', which Whittle duly submitted to the commanding officer of *Ark Royal*. This described a type of self-propelled launching trolley with a built-in engine that Whittle believed would be an improvement over the catapult arrangement then in use, which was driven by an explosive charge. Whittle also thought that the self-propelled trolley arrangement would have an advantage by doing away with all the wire ropes and pulleys that were part of the standard catapult arrangement. Although this was no doubt a novel suggestion, his commanding officer turned it down, perhaps realising that new aircraft carrier designs were on the horizon and would likely have a much different arrangement for launching aircraft compared to the rather rudimentary facilities on *Ark Royal*.

Whittle's work as a test pilot in these challenging and dangerous conditions was recognised in the usual understated manner of official communications of the time. The commanding officer of *Ark Royal* wrote to the Vice-Admiral, Commanding, Reserve Fleet, as follows:

> I wish to bring to the notice of their lordships the very satisfactory work carried out by Flying Officer F. Whittle, RAF, attached to HMS *Ark Royal* from Marine Aircraft Establishment, Felixstowe, for the present trials. This officer made a total of 47 catapult launches under varying conditions during the series, and in addition carried out a forced landing flotation test in most realistic conditions and in a praiseworthy manner. His services have been invaluable and his airmanship inspired confidence in all concerned in the trials. His skill as a pilot and in float plane handling by making up to nine successive catapult launches in one day enabled conclusive results to be obtained in the minimum time.[11]

Whittle also received hints that he might be given an award such as the AFC (Air Force Cross) for his dedicated and dangerous work at Felixstowe. This award is intended to recognise 'an act or acts of valour, courage or devotion to duty whilst flying, though not in active operations against the enemy'.

In the end, nothing came of this and Whittle believed that it may have been, at least in part, due to the somewhat unfortunate incident that saw Flt Lieutenant Kirk leave the cockpit in an 'unauthorised manner'.

During the eighteen months he spent at Felixstowe, Whittle continued to work on his jet engine concept in his limited spare time. He also wrote a number of letters to industrialists and academics describing his new invention, and asking them for advice on how he might commercialise it. Most of the firms he wrote to, if they responded at all, would indicate that they had no interest in his novel concepts. Still not completely discouraged, Whittle would often have discussions about his new concept with his fellow pilots in the officers' mess, but most of his colleagues didn't really understand the completely novel ideas that he was working on. One exception to this was Rolf Dudley-Williams, who had shared a hut with Whittle during their student days at RAF Cranwell. Williams had been exposed to some of Whittle's novel ideas during their time at Cranwell, and was pleased to be reunited with him at Felixstowe.

Chapter 4

Back to School – RAF Henlow and Cambridge University

After four years of general duties every RAF officer was expected to take further training in one of four specialised areas: navigation, armament, signals, or engineering. Whittle naturally chose engineering and with strong backing from his superior officers was assigned in 1932 to take the engineering course at RAF Henlow. This station had been established as a major aircraft repair centre, and the RAF Officers Engineering School was also opened there in 1927. Whittle was the perfect candidate for the engineering course, as he had both the very practical background and experience resulting from working in his father's machine shop and from his RAF apprenticeship, as well as the substantial theoretical knowledge of engineering he gained from his self-study related to jet propulsion. As a result, he proved to be an outstanding candidate and was awarded an overall grade of 98 per cent in his studies.

Prior to about 1930 the practice had been to send one or two of the top graduates from the engineering course at Henlow for further study at Cambridge University. However, just before Whittle started his studies at Henlow this practice had been discontinued as the feeling was that the largely theoretical work done at Cambridge was not particularly useful for the RAF. Given his outstanding performance, however, and the realisation that he was very much a gifted candidate, the practice was revised for Whittle and he was sent to Cambridge to do the three-year engineering 'tripos', as the degree course is still called today. The origin of the term tripos is somewhat obscure, but is said to originate from the three-legged stool that examination candidates were required to sit on when undergoing oral examinations in the medieval university. Even today most courses consist of 'preliminary' examinations at the end of each of the first two years, while successful completion of the final tripos exams results in a degree. In any event, Whittle was delighted because he knew that there were professors at Cambridge who would be able to enhance his knowledge, particularly in the field of fluid dynamics, which he realised was critical for a better understanding of the performance of his jet propulsion concepts.

Although the engineering degree course, like most courses at Cambridge, consisted of three years of study, Whittle was told he should just undertake the final two years and then take the tripos exams in Mechanical Sciences. Even to Whittle this seemed rather daunting, as he realised that all of his theoretical knowledge was entirely self-taught and he had no experience of university studies. However, his superiors had high confidence in his abilities, and perhaps also had an eye to having him return to active service as soon as possible. Whittle began his studies in 1934, graduating in 1936 with a Bachelor of Arts degree (still the first degree awarded to all Cambridge graduates, irrespective of the field of study). This was no doubt a challenging time for Whittle, as he now had a wife and two young sons to support. However, his superior officers had their confidence in him fully confirmed when he was awarded a first-class degree; not an easy feat.

Like all students at Cambridge, Whittle was formally admitted to one of the constituent colleges that make up the university. He chose the oldest, Peterhouse. This small college was founded in 1284 by the Bishop of Ely, and is situated conveniently in the centre of Cambridge and close to the engineering laboratories. Most undergraduates would arrive directly from secondary school aged 18 and were expected to live in college, which provided accommodation. As Whittle was much older, and recently married, he was given special dispensation to live outside college. He was able to find rental accommodation for his wife and himself in the small village of Trumpington, just on the edge of Cambridge and conveniently located near to the engineering laboratories. Whittle was still expected, however, to take part in college activities such as 'supervisions' (tutorial sessions), and to attend some of the special dinners, or 'feasts', held in the college.

Each college consists of a number of fellows, or senior academics, and is presided over by a master. The master is usually a particularly distinguished academic, or in some cases a non-academic who has achieved great distinction in another field, such as the diplomatic service, the church or the military. During Whittle's time at Cambridge the Master of Peterhouse was Sir William Birdwood, who had been given a baronetcy (a hereditary form of knighthood) in 1919. Birdwood was an outstanding soldier, had been a field marshal in the First World War, and later on became Commander-in-Chief, India, in the British Army. As someone who had great respect for the military in general, and for distinguished careers in particular, Whittle would have been delighted to receive a letter from Birdwood in June 1936 congratulating him on the award of a first-class degree.

Birdwood wrote: 'I am so glad to be able to congratulate you on behalf of the College, as I do most heartily, on the first class you have just taken in Mechanical Sciences. This takes with it the very best of good wishes to you for all success for years to come.'[12]

Two years later Birdwood was further honoured by being elevated to the House of Lords as the first Baron Birdwood. During his time at Cambridge, Whittle continued to work on his jet engine concepts, and had many discussions with senior academics in the engineering department about his design. In particular he spoke to Professor Bennett Melvill Jones, who taught at Cambridge for more than thirty years.

Partway through his undergraduate studies Whittle had made a critical decision that was to have a profound effect on the commercialisation of the jet engine and any profits that he may have made from his discovery. In early 1935 he received a letter from the Air Ministry, to whom he had assigned the rights to his original jet propulsion patent, reminding him that the patent renewal fees were due. The letter also pointed out that there would be no official funds available to pay the £5 required for the renewal, and it would be up to Whittle to make the payment if he wished to avoid having the patent lapse. With a wife and two young sons to support on a rather meagre RAF officer's salary, Whittle thought that he could not justify spending such a sum to renew his patent rights. This decision was also taken, in part, in the knowledge that he had spent a great deal of time in trying to get official and commercial backing for his ideas, with little success. Although many people, and a few companies, had expressed interest in the concept, none of them had been willing to get involved financially in supporting the long and arduous programme of work that they believed would inevitably be required to bring ultimate success to such an ambitious project. As a result, Whittle decided against paying the £5, and allowed the patent to lapse. The result of this crucial decision was that anyone, in any country, would now be free to commercialise the jet engine if they felt so inclined.

Ironically, just a few months after letting his patent lapse, Whittle received a letter from his friend Rolf Dudley-Williams. He had retained a very clear recollection of Whittle's enthusiastic description of his jet propulsion concept and often relayed this to acquaintances. Dudley-Williams was trying to make his way in business, and had set up a small company, General Enterprises, with a friend, James Collingwood Burdett Tinling (usually referred to as JCB Tinling), known to his friends as 'Col'. Tinling was the older brother of Ted Tinling, who would go on to find fame as a tennis fashion designer.

Dudley-Williams and Tinling's first venture was the design and manufacture of an automated vending machine intended to dispense cigarettes. Tinling had also been an RAF officer and pilot, but was invalided out following a mid-air collision and subsequent crash of his aeroplane, which resulted in a permanent leg injury. He became very interested in Whittle's concept and urged Dudley-Williams to set up a meeting with him. The three former RAF pilots had much in common, and quickly formed a strong friendship cemented by the belief that a new aero engine concept would revolutionise not only military but also commercial aviation. Although Whittle told Dudley-Williams and Tinling that he had let his original patent lapse, they both believed that there would be sufficient scope for additional patents around the basic concept to protect Whittle's intellectual property.

As a result of their meeting in Cambridge in mid-1935, the three partners decided to form a company to pursue the jet engine project. Dudley-Williams and Tinling did not have much money themselves, but agreed that they would try to raise at least £50,000 (£950,000 in today's terms) to finance the design and development of a prototype engine, ready for testing in an aeroplane. In return for raising the funds for development it was agreed that Dudley-Williams and Tinling would each receive a 25 per cent interest in any company formed to pursue the engine development. Tinling approached yet another ex-RAF pilot, Mogens L. Bramson, who had also trained as an aeronautical engineer to see if he could help with their project. Bramson, in turn, introduced the three partners to a relatively small London investment bank, O.T. Falk and Partners, which he thought might be interested in funding such a risky development. One of the directors of O.T. Falk was Sir Maurice Bonham-Carter, a well-connected and Oxford-educated barrister who had been parliamentary private secretary to Herbert Henry Asquith, leader of the Liberal Party and Prime Minister from 1908 to 1916.

Coincidentally, Bonham-Carter was also the great grandfather of Helena Bonham-Carter, the well-known present-day actress.

Oswald Falk had been a colleague of John Maynard Keynes at the Treasury before leaving to start his own investment bank. Together with Keynes, Falk had made a good deal of money speculating in the currency markets, and had left the Treasury to set up his investment bank, which was designed to invest primarily in new business concerns with potentially high returns but which also carried high risk. To help sort out the wheat from the chaff, he often employed technical specialists to provide careful assessments of his potential investments. One of these was Lancelot Law Whyte, a Cambridge-educated physicist with wide-ranging interests in both technology and the philosophy of science. Whyte was the son of Dr Alexander Whyte, a Presbyterian minister. He was educated at Trinity College, where he studied physics under Ernest Rutherford, who had emigrated from New Zealand to the UK. Rutherford had a great reputation as an experimental physicist, and was known as the 'father of nuclear physics'. Although not widely known in the UK, after the Second World War Whyte became a well-known author of books on the history and philosophy of science.

In September 1935, Bramson duly arranged a meeting for Whittle, Tinling and Dudley-Williams with Whyte and Bonham-Carter at O.T. Falk and Partners. Whyte quickly grasped Whittle's concept and as a result of these discussions he prepared a favourable report on the prospects for the jet propulsion venture. O.T. Falk and Partners then engaged Bramson to prepare a more detailed report on Whittle's proposed engine design in order that they may make an informed investment decision. This brief report, known in later years just as the 'Bramson Report', gave a favourable review of Whittle's concept, which ultimately led to the successful development of his dream and changed the nature of aviation forever.[13]

Although providing a good summary of the benefits of jet propulsion and a clear description of each of the main components, in retrospect the report was incredibly naïve about the major obstacle to the successful realisation of Whittle's dream. In his main conclusions, Bramson noted that, 'His fundamental discovery is that the gas turbine, though very inefficient as a prime mover when power is required in the form of shaft horse-power, can be adequately efficient as an auxiliary to the production of a power jet.' The report, dated October 1935, contained just six pages, but the section describing the crucial challenges of combustion read as follows in its entirety:

Combustion Chamber and Burners
These do not call for special comment and any minor problems arising should yield to ordinary skilled design.

This was the only mention of combustion in Bramson's report, which only in hindsight is surprising. In reality the main obstacle to the ultimately successful development of Whittle's engine was the design of a combustion chamber that could sustain the very high combustion intensity required. The difficulties to come with the combustion system were not yet known, of course, and Bramson's report ended with very brief recommendations, which read in full:

Recommendations
The 'Brief Outline of Development Procedure' appended to this Report (Appendix III) has, by request, been prepared by the inventor.

I recommend the adoption of the procedure herein proposed with the proviso that all designs should be submitted to an independent authority on turbine and compressor design before actual construction is undertaken.

It was then on the basis of these very brief recommendations that the development of what would turn out to be a complete revolution in aircraft propulsion began in earnest. The report convinced O.T. Falk and Partners to support Whittle's bold new ideas and they agreed to invest in his work.

Negotiations in early 1936 led to the so-called 'Four-Party Agreement', which set up a company to be called Power Jets Ltd, with the shareholders being Whittle as one party, Dudley-Williams and Tinling as the second, O.T. Falk and Partners, to be represented by Whyte and Bramson, as the third party, and finally the President of the Air Council being the fourth, given that Whittle was still a serving officer in the RAF. Whittle, Tinling and Dudley-Williams together would hold 49 per cent of the shares as the 'A' shareholders, while O.T. Falk and Partners would hold the remaining (and controlling) 51 per cent share as 'B' shareholders. The agreement stated that O.T. Falk and Partners would put up £2,000 initially and commit to a further £18,000 over the next eighteen months.

In return for this, Whittle would turn over all of his patent rights in the engine to the company, although of course his initial key patent had lapsed and was now open for anyone to exploit. However, Whittle was able to convince the investors that there would be scope to develop other, subsidiary patents that would enable the company to keep control of the technology. He had already been working on several of these, and had three patent applications just about ready to be filed. The agreement further stated the original shareholdings would not be diluted until a total of £50,000 had been invested. The company was incorporated in March 1936, with the directors being named as Tinling and Dudley-Williams representing 'A shareholders' and Whyte and Bonham-Carter representing the 'B shareholders'. Whyte was named as the chairman, Bramson was to be an official 'consultant' and finally Whittle was named as 'honorary chief engineer', given that he was still very much a serving RAF officer. By special agreement with the Air Ministry, Whittle was given special dispensation to spend 'no more than six hours per week' working on the jet propulsion proposal.[14] This provision, of course, turned out to have little effect as Whittle essentially worked seven days per week on the new engine, with only a few interruptions due to ill health, from then until the end of his career in the RAF in 1948.

Of course, at this time Whittle was still pursuing his undergraduate studies, and preparing for his final exams in early 1936. Nevertheless, with some funding now in place he began to work on the detailed design of an experimental engine and started looking for a manufacturing firm that might be able to build a prototype suitable for testing. As the jet engine was so different from anything then in production, there were not many suitable candidate firms. However, now with some funding in place, Whittle again approached the British Thomson-Houston (BTH) company in Rugby, with whom he had first met some five years earlier. He proposed that they be engaged to build prototype jet engine components for him on a cost-plus basis. This they readily agreed to do, and they provided an initial quote of £1,700 plus 30 per cent for profit and overhead to manufacture all of the components required for a complete prototype engine. In addition, the company agreed to provide Whittle with some space in their large factory to enable him to assemble his prototype engine and begin testing it. He was also able to engage BTH detail design engineers on an as-needed basis as well as the mechanics and technicians required for the assembly and testing work.

Over the next two years Whittle would become a well-recognised figure in the BTH factory, and developed some strong friendships with senior engineers there. These included the chief engineer, Henry (known as Harry) Sporborg, an American who had come from the General Electric (GE) heavy manufacturing division in the USA in 1902 to help establish the turbine factory, and who ultimately became chairman of BTH in 1944. Also, the chief turbine engineer Frederick Samuelson, as well as his deputy, R. Collingham, were directly involved in working with Whittle to put his dreams into practice. Samuelson had been employed by BTH since 1897 and was in charge of the turbine engineering department from 1903. Early in his career he had been sent to the US to learn about steam turbine design at GE, and upon his return he became one of the leaders in this area in the UK. Plate 9 shows the extended team of employees who were ultimately involved in the design and test work undertaken in the BTH factory under contract to Power Jets.

Despite spending only two years studying for his degree, and working nearly full-time on developing his novel engine concept, Whittle graduated in 1936 with a first-class degree. His tutor, Roy Lubbock, was a fellow at Peterhouse for more than years and was also a lecturer in engineering with strong connections to senior government officials. Lubbock came from an aristocratic family with a strong scientific background, as his grandfather was Sir John Lubbock, 3rd Baronet, who had been Vice-President of the Royal Society. Roy Lubbock was very impressed with Whittle's abilities and the work he was able to do on his engine concept while still pursuing his degree course. He also recognised that Whittle's work on the engine would greatly benefit by continuing the kind of collaboration he had developed with academics at Cambridge, such as Professor Melvill Jones, and others. As a result, he was able to convince senior RAF officers that they should make special arrangements to enable Whittle to continue on at Cambridge for a post-graduate year to continue work on his engine. Whittle was then given special dispensation to remain for the academic year 1936–37. During this time he worked with Melvill Jones on aerodynamic research, much of which was related directly to the operation of his engine concept.

The timing of Whittle's post-graduate year also very neatly coincided with the successful completion of negotiations with O.T. Falk and Partners to provide the much-needed funding to build a prototype engine. In effect it meant that Whittle was pretty well free to work nearly full-time on getting an experimental engine designed and built with the help of engineers from BTH in Rugby. In addition, Whittle spent a great deal of time shuttling back and forth between Cambridge and the BTH factory in Rugby, where components for his prototype engine were being manufactured. The very first prototype became known as the 'WU' (short for 'Whittle Unit'), with no reference to it being an engine of any kind. This was largely to do with security concerns so that if any of the increasing number of BTH employees working on the engine were overheard discussing their work outside the factory no one would be likely to learn what they were actually doing.

Towards the end of 1936 Whittle received the first indication that there might be some government funding available to help with the development of his new engine concept. Whyte, now the chairman of Power Jets, received a letter in late October from David Pye, the Assistant Director of Engine Research in the Air Ministry, indicating that the Aeronautical Research Committee might be prepared to recommend to the Ministry that they should provide some financial assistance towards the increasing costs of research and development of the 'unit'. In return for the proposed funding the Air Ministry told Whittle that he should be prepared to turn over 35 per cent of his 'A' shares in Power Jets to the Air Council.

During this period, while BTH were manufacturing components, Whittle used his time to write down in detail his thinking behind the design of his novel new engine. This resulted in a forty-page document, entitled 'The Theories and Inventions forming the basis of Developments by Power Jets Ltd.', which was dated October 1936.

At the beginning of the report Whittle summarised the objectives of the 'programme' to be:

a) To produce a propulsion unit which will make possible the achievement of high speed flight in the stratosphere.
b) Eventually to produce a successful gas turbine.

Whittle then went on to say 'it is hoped that objective (b) will follow as a natural consequence of progress in achieving the first objective'. The report also included a section on 'Design Data for the first Unit', and some photographs.

Shortly after Whittle's report was submitted, another document was sent to the Air Ministry by Dr A.A. Griffith of the Royal Aircraft Establishment. Griffith had evidently been asked by the Ministry to put down his independent views of Whittle's proposed new propulsion concept. Griffith gave his views of the possible advantages and disadvantages of Whittle's new concept compared to the turbo-propellor concept, which was under development by Griffith himself at the time. The 'turbo-prop' design makes use of the hot high-pressure gases exiting the first turbine stage used to drive the compressor to drive a secondary turbine, which is connected directly to a conventional propeller. This concept of the 'gas turbine engine' had been pioneered by Griffith in his work for the Air Ministry, and a working prototype was built in 1928. After initial testing, however, Griffith's design was not pursued commercially at that time due to its relatively poor performance compared to well-developed aircraft piston engines such as those built by Rolls-Royce and other manufacturers.

Griffith's report, entitled 'Report on the Whittle Jet Propulsion System', was submitted to the Air Ministry in February 1937. Overall it appeared to be fair, but the conclusions were somewhat disappointing to Whittle and his Power Jets team. Griffith stated,

'In its present form, the proposed system is not suitable for economic flight involving stringent take-off requirements. It has advantages in certain special circumstances where take-off is not a problem and low specific weight is more important than low specific fuel consumption.' Whittle was naturally upset by the conclusions of the report, and he and his team prepared a rebuttal. This seemed to have the desired effect, and Whittle and his team continued to receive support from the Air Ministry.

The design of a suitable combustion chamber was something that Whittle had not spent much time thinking about, and was an area where he had little knowledge. As a result, during his postgraduate year he visited a number of combustion specialists with a view to getting their assistance with the problem of manufacturing a new combustion chamber with a 'combustion intensity' many times higher than anything then in existence.

One of the people he approached at a trade fair was Mr A. Laidlaw of the specialist firm Laidlaw Drew and Co. located in Leith, an industrial area just outside Edinburgh. This small firm specialised in manufacturing oil burners and combustion equipment for industrial applications, such as glass manufacturing and refuse incineration. Although Laidlaw was astonished to learn that the combustion intensity Whittle was looking for was far higher than anything then available, he agreed to design a combustor that should be suitable for the WU engine. As a result, a single large combustor was designed to burn fuel oil at a rate much higher than had been achieved to date. The company also manufactured the prototype burner and delivered it to Rugby for assembly with the compressor and turbine units that had been built by BTH. Laidlaw Drew and Co. remained in business until 2006, when it was purchased by the American company Eclipse, a major manufacturer of industrial combustion equipment.

In early 1937 BTH had assembled all the components of the WU prototype engine according to the engineering drawings supplied by

Whittle. These included the centrifugal compressor and the turbine assembly mounted on a common shaft, as well as the combustion chamber supplied by Laidlaw Drew and Co. Whittle had found an old car engine, which was to be used as a starter to provide initial rotation of the compressor-turbine assembly. In the end this did not prove powerful enough, and was substituted with a 20kW electric motor, which had the advantage of having high torque at low speed. BTH also allocated a small space at the end of one of their large steam turbine assembly halls for testing the prototype.

The first trial of the engine that would eventually revolutionise aviation took place on 12 April 1937, with Whittle at the controls and a small group of BTH mechanics as helpers. Collingham, the senior BTH turbine engineer, insisted that there should not be a large crowd of 'observers', as the potential danger of a turbine or compressor wheel bursting during an 'overspeed' event was well known. As it turned out, Collingham's concerns were well founded and the initial engine run proved to be a much more exhilarating event than most had expected. Whittle's description of the excitement in the factory after the engine first started clearly comes through in his recollections of the event:

> For a second or two the speed of the engine increased slowly, and then, with a rising shriek like an air-raid siren, the speed began to rise rapidly and large patches of red heat became visible on the combustion chamber casing. The engine was obviously out of control. All of the BTH personnel, realising what this meant, went down the factory at high speed in varying directions. A few of them took refuge in nearby large steam turbine exhaust casings, which made useful shelters.
>
> I screwed down the control valve immediately, but this had no effect and the speed continued to rise, but fortunately the acceleration ceased at about 8,000 rpm and slowly the

revs dropped again. Needless to say, this incident did not do my nervous system any good at all. I have rarely been so frightened.[15]

After this very exciting start another attempt was made the following day, but once again ended with an engine 'runaway' event and BTH personnel scuttling away to hiding places on the factory floor. Eventually the problem was found to be the pooling of fuel in the bottom of the combustion chamber, which then continued to burn well after Whittle had shut off the main fuel supply valve. The tests proved, however, that Whittle's ideas were correct, and that this would be the basis of a whole new direction in aircraft propulsion. There has likely never been such an exciting time for a young engineer so soon after graduating from university.

Chapter 5

The 'Special Duty List'

At the end of his post-graduate year in July 1937, and on the basis of the first running of the WU engine, the Air Ministry decided to allow Whittle to work full-time on developing a practical propulsion unit suitable for use in fighter planes.

This was done by placing him on the 'Special Duty List' and assigning him to work full-time with the small Power Jets team and the BTH personnel contracted to them. In retrospect this was an enlightened decision, and shows that even with war on the horizon, and the need for a rapid build-up of armed forces, the Air Ministry could make allowances for someone they realised had special talents. This enabled Whittle to make a unique contribution, although ultimately the successful development of a practical jet engine was just too late to make a significant impact on the war effort. It did, however, place Britain into the forefront of a whole new industry in which it retains a leadership role to this day through Rolls-Royce Holdings plc and a wide variety of suppliers.

After the initial runs of the WU engine, the senior BTH engineers decided that the testing was too risky for their turbine hall, and proposed a move for Whittle and his small team, which now consisted of a number of BTH personnel on secondment. They suggested that trials be moved to a small BTH foundry, called the Ladywood Works and located in Lutterworth, that was no longer in use. This was only about 8 miles from the Rugby factory, and turned out to be quite a suitable site for further testing of the WU engine and later variants.

After the successful start-up of the WU prototype, the Air Ministry became more convinced of the prospects for jet propulsion, and agreed to provide some research funding to support the move into the Ladywood Works, and provide some badly needed renovation money to allow it to be made suitable for engine testing. This also enabled Whittle to begin to hire a few designers and technicians as full-time Power Jets employees, gradually reducing the need to rely solely on BTH for these services. The small Power Jets team moved into the Ladywood Works at the beginning of 1938 after some initial clean-up of the former foundry site had been carried out, and they began to prepare for further engine testing. Funding was to continue to be an issue, however, as O.T. Falk and Partners were not prepared to provide the level that was initially agreed with the Power Jets principals.

As a result, the ownership of Power Jets reverted to the 'A' shareholders, Whittle, Williams and Tinling, while BTH agreed to invest some £2,500 in the project. Also, the Air Ministry, under the auspices of the Director of Scientific Research, agreed to provide a research contract of £5,000 to Power Jets. Whittle was kept very busy not only supervising the engine testing and analysing test run data, but also with the preliminary design of new variants of the WU engine and future development models.

In all of this work Whittle was still working with BTH engineers under contract to provide most of the detailed design drawings needed for manufacturing. He had a good relationship in general with the BTH employees and effectively had the run of the engineering office, with the ability to call on individual designers for work on specific components. Somewhat unfortunately, this began to change in late 1937 when Whittle began scrutinising the detailed design of turbine blades that had been done by some of the BTH engineers. In checking the inlet and outlet angles of the turbine stator blades specified on the drawings, he realised that they would produce 'solid body' rotation of the flow in which the angular velocity varied directly with the radius. This was quite contrary to what Whittle had always assumed to be best practice, as early on he had read Stodola's excellent treatise on turbine design, and realised that for best efficiency the blade angles should provide a 'free-vortex' flow pattern. This is similar to the flow pattern in a natural vortex, such as the flow of water down a sink drain, in which the radial flow velocity increases towards the centre of the flow pattern. The free-vortex flow, Whittle realised, would result in the optimum distribution of gases in the turbine, resulting in the highest possible efficiency. When he asked the BTH Chief turbine engineer, Samuelson, and his deputy, Collingham, about this it became clear that they had never heard of the benefits of free-vortex blade design, and had always used the principle of solid-body flow in their blade designs. This disagreement on fundamental turbine design issues was the start of significant distrust between Whittle and his BTH colleagues, which was only made worse when Whittle submitted a patent for free-vortex gas turbine blade design. From then on the working relationship between Whittle and BTH was rather fragile, and left Whittle determined to recruit as much 'in-house' expertise in the small Power Jets staff as possible. Fortunately, this was made easier by the build-up of facilities and staff at the Ladywood Works, which greatly reduced the need to rely on BTH personnel.

With the end of his post-graduate year at Cambridge, and now his full-time assignment to continue with jet engine development, Whittle decided to move closer to where the development was taking place. In mid-October 1937 he moved his family from Trumpington to a house, called Broomfield, on Bilton road in Rugby, which was rented by Power Jets. This greatly reduced the amount of travelling time, and enabled him to move quickly between the BTH design office, where detailed design work was still being done under contract, and the Ladywood Works, where all testing was to be done.

During the lull in testing necessitated by the move from the BTH factory to the Ladywood Works the original WU engine was rebuilt with the aim of improving reliability and performance.

Since the beginning of testing there had been three main failures of the engine, and after each the powerplant was redesigned in order to improve reliability and performance. The first version had first run on 12 April 1937 and testing continued until August. The second version then first ran in early 1938 and provided much valuable data until it was severely damaged by a compressor impeller failure in April 1939. By mid-1939 it had become clear to the Air Ministry that Whittle's engine was going to be a viable alternative to the near ubiquitous Rolls-Royce Merlin piston engine. Whittle told colleagues that Hayne Constant, who had been seconded to the Air Ministry from his position at Imperial College, said that the 'unit' was no longer a long-term development exercise but a 'production job'. Constant, also a Cambridge University engineering graduate, would go on to join Power Jets in 1944 as Director of Research and Development, and ultimately became Director of the National Gas Turbine Establishment (NGTE) from 1946 to 1960.

The third version of Whittle's engine ran from September 1939 until it was destroyed by a turbine failure. This marked the end of testing with the original WU design, and although there had been several mechanical failures, it had completely validated Whittle's novel concept for jet propulsion. Whittle and his growing team then redesigned the engine to build on the success of the very first prototype, resulting in several newer versions that became known as the W1 and W2 types. These designs were also improved continuously as a result of the increasing amount of test data being obtained. Whittle also continued to make detailed improvements to the engine design, and met with BTH designers to show them his new 'fir-tree root' design for attaching individual turbine blades to the turbine disc. This was designed to replace the usual 'bulb' type of attachment that had always been used by turbine manufacturers. This was designed to increase the surface area of the blade attachment point with the turbine disc, resulting in reduced stresses. It proved to be much stronger and more reliable than the bulb design, and would ultimately become the standard attachment used by all manufacturers to secure both turbine and compressor blades to their respective discs. Meanwhile, Whittle's rather brusque manner was summarised in an annual report for 1939 by Air Vice-Marshal Roderic Hill, who described Whittle's 'ability in duties now engaged', and 'zeal in performance of duties' as 'Exceptional'. However, he also noted that Whittle's 'tact in handling of men' was 'Average'!

An early experimental version of the redesigned engine, known as the W1X, first ran in early 1940 and was then sent in October 1941 to the GE Company in the US. This important step marked the very beginning of jet engine design and manufacturing by what has now become one of the largest jet engine companies in the world.

Combustion continued to be the main obstacle to attaining the ability to run at the full-load design speed for sustained periods of time. This was quite ironic, given that Bramson's only comment about combustion issues in his initial evaluation of Whittle's engine, was 'these do not call for special comment and any minor problems arising should yield to ordinary skilled design, as we have seen'.[16] Whittle had been grappling with this for the best part of two years, and had tried many different combustion chamber configurations in order to provide reliable ignition and control of the combustion of the kerosene fuel being used. He had realised early on that the use of one large combustion chamber was not conducive to the goal of achieving a compact engine design or even distribution of combustion gases to the complete turbine rotor. He soon settled on a set of ten much smaller combustion chambers, distributed around the circumference of the engine. This was successful in improving the distribution of hot gases to the turbine, but it was still difficult to achieve reliable ignition and combustion over a wide range of operating conditions, which necessitated wide variation in the overall air–fuel ratio.

One of the most difficult problems in the novel new engine design was the very high combustion intensity required in order to produce as much heat as possible in the very small space between the compressor and the turbine. This led Whittle to an ingenious design in which the flow in the combustion chambers was 'reversed', in that ductwork was provided to direct air from the compressor outlet to the rear of the engine, where it went through a 90° turn to enter the flame tube, and then the combustion gases were reversed through 90° again to emerge in their original direction through the turbine wheel, as can be seen in Plate 11.[17] However, the evaporator tubing, used to vaporise all the fuel before it could be mixed with air and then ignited, often suffered from 'coking' due to the very high temperatures. The engine would have to be stopped after a few minutes of running in order to clean out the evaporator tubing before being restarted. This became a very frustrating problem, and Whittle spent almost two years struggling to improve combustion reliability and intensity. This was finally solved following consultations with Isaac Lubbock of the Asiatic Petroleum company, at that time a part of the Shell Oil group of companies. Lubbock, also an engineering graduate from Cambridge, had been working on very high-intensity combustion systems for liquid-fuelled rockets at the Shell combustion laboratory in Fulham. He had eventually designed a simple combustion system in which liquid fuel was sprayed into the combustion chamber at very high pressure, resulting in atomisation of the fuel into very small droplets. These droplets, due to their high surface to volume ratio, would then evaporate rapidly and mix with the surrounding air to form a combustible mixture. This mixture could then be readily ignited by a simple electrical ignitor, which operates much like a conventional spark plug.

Following extensive discussions with Lubbock, Whittle redesigned the combustion chamber to incorporate the novel atomising combustion system developed by Lubbock and his team at Shell. The new combustor design finally provided very reliable ignition and combustion of all of the fuel without coking. It also resulted in a much higher combustion intensity than with the previous version that was designed to vaporise all the fuel before it was ignited. One very big advantage of this new design was that combustion could be sustained over a very wide range of overall air-fuel ratios, as it is the local air-fuel ratio surrounding each rapidly evaporating droplet that determines the ignitability of the mixture. In other words, each droplet would behave independently and would ignite when sufficient fuel had evaporated to form a locally combustible mixture. When Whittle and his team went ahead and redesigned their burners to provide atomisation of the fuel, the resulting ignition reliability and combustion stability seemed miraculous. Almost overnight the two years of frustration with combustion issues had disappeared and this marked a real turning point for the success of Whittle's endeavours. Much later Whittle commented that, 'The introduction of the Shell system may be said to mark the point where combustion ceased to be an obstacle of development.'[18]

Plate 11 shows a simple line drawing of the final version of Whittle's WU engine, which was the workhorse of his early development work. In this drawing there is no connection shown between the compressor outlet on the right and the stub pipe entering the combustion chambers, but the arrangement can be more clearly seen in the photograph of Plate 12.[19] The small car engine used as a starting motor can also be seen in Plate 12, together with the motorcycle fuel tank in the foreground used to fuel the starter engine. The arrangement of the reverse-flow combustion chambers for the WU engine, and its later variants, was later criticised by others for being unnecessarily complex, resulting in high pressure losses. However, it was a clever way to increase the combustion volume in order to reduce the combustion intensity as much as possible and had the added advantage of providing a very compact overall engine. This also meant that only a short central shaft was required to connect the turbine to the compressor, eliminating the need for any central support bearings.

As knowledge of the success of Whittle's new engine concept spread to government laboratories and other manufacturing firms, many suggestions for improvements to the basic engine design were put forward. Perhaps the most important of these were the proposals to utilise an axial-flow compressor design and 'annular' combustion chambers. Although both of these concepts would eventually prove to be the best approach for powerful and compact engines, Whittle was at first reluctant to adapt these techniques to his own designs. Researchers at RAE Farnborough, for example, wrote to Power Jets towards the end of 1939 to outline the shortcomings of centrifugal compressors. They also put forward an argument in favour of a much more compact annular combustion chamber, which would ultimately prove to be much more effective than the 'double reverse flow' approach that was a hallmark of Whittle's early designs. In later years, as much more compact combustion chambers have been developed, most jet engines have ended up with 'inline' combustion chambers, which result in lower pressure loss but a substantially longer engine.

By early 1940 the Air Ministry was finally beginning to take notice of the radical new engine, and a regular stream of very senior visitors began to arrive to see for themselves what Whittle had accomplished. At the end of January Air Vice-Marshal Tedder visited the Ladywood Works, and after seeing the engine running said that he 'will do all he can to help on the development'. Whittle was also quite taken aback when Tedder asked if Power Jets could produce ten engines per week! Whyte then told the air marshal that Power Jets had plans for a new development works, and Tedder seemed to be 'strongly in favour' of this according to Whittle's notes of the meeting. He also told Whittle that the Air Ministry 'intended to take a much greater interest in Power Jets'. At the end of his visit he also said that he would telephone Mr Sporborg at BTH and urge him 'to get on with the job'. As an interesting aside, Henry Tizard visited a few days before to brief Whittle and his team about the upcoming visit by Tedder. In a foretaste of the far future of aerial warfare, Whittle suggested to Tizard that the Ministry should also be considering an 'automatically controlled pilot-less aeroplane'. Whittle recorded that Tizard did not completely ignore this suggestion, but suggested that perhaps it should be left 'for the next war'!

Following the visit by Tedder, David Pye, now promoted to Director of Scientific Research at the Air Ministry, wrote to BTH chief engineer Harry Sporborg, asking him to expedite the manufacturing of a number of Whittle's new engine prototypes. He wrote:

Whittle Jet Propulsion Engines
You have for some considerable time been associated with the research being carried out by Power Jets Limited on the Whittle engine, the position being, I believe, that all the design work and manufacturing processes are carried out in your Rugby drawing offices and workshops.

During the last few months of this research the results obtained have been extremely promising, and the Air Ministry have now decided that further engines should be built on a high priority. In these days it is appreciated that in any work of this description considerable delays are likely to occur both in the delivery of materials and in machining processes due to the pressure of other urgent Government work, but I hope that if you are fully aware of the great importance that the Air

Ministry attach to the development of this Whittle engine you will take all steps in your power to ensure that no unnecessary delay occurs in the completion of these engines and that you will do all you can to assist Power Jets Limited in their work.

In this connection a suggestion has been made by this firm that a great saving of time should be effected if your Engineer, Mr Randels, and the three draughtsmen who are wholly engaged on work connected with the Whittle engines could be transferred to the Ladywood Works where the design could then be concentrated under Squadron Leader Whittle's personal attention. It is also very desirable that arrangements should be made for the engines to be assembled at the Ladywood Works. In addition to the saving of time and increase in efficiency that would result from these changes there is also the question of security which arises and it does appear undesirable that drawings which contain essential information relative to the Whittle engine should be kept in two places, as at present; the Ladywood Works and your Rugby factory.

It will therefore be appreciated if you will consider the foregoing suggestions and let me know in due course what arrangements to this end you are able to make.

I am, Gentlemen,
Your obedient Servant,

D.R. Pye
Director of Scientific Research

Whittle paid a visit to RAE Farnborough in the middle of February 1940, to meet with research staff there and to learn about the work they were doing on a revised version of his engine. He was shown a drawing of an engine design incorporating an axial-flow compressor, which was only half the diameter of the radial-flow, or centrifugal compressor that Whittle's design incorporated. He realised that using the axial-flow compressor design would make the engine much smaller in diameter, which would be advantageous, particularly if two engines were to be installed under the wings. He had invested so much time and effort into improving the performance of his single-stage centrifugal compressor design, however, that he could not readily come around to the view that the axial-flow type might be the better choice. Although he could readily see the advantages of the axial-flow compressor, he also knew that much more development work was likely to be needed before it would have the pressure ratio of his centrifugal design, with the high efficiency needed for a successful engine. Over time, however, rapid development of the axial-flow compressor led to it being the design choice for nearly all jet engines, particularly the most powerful ones.

During this period there was considerable discussion between government officials, Whittle and the various aircraft and engine manufacturers to determine which company might be best placed to begin manufacturing jet engines in quantity. BTH were still one of the companies in the running, and Sporborg said that they could build eight of Whittle's W2 design engines by the end of 1940. He also said, however, that if they did not get a contract for eight engines they would prefer to not go on with the job at all. BTH personnel were also annoyed when they learned that some Power Jets staff had expressed the opinion that 'the BTH turbine factory was unsuited for small work of this kind'. In the end, of course, they were likely correct, as both the facilities and staff at BTH were used to working on very heavy steam turbine components, in which 'the heavier the better' seemed to be the right approach for reliability and longevity. This approach, however, was quite the opposite of what was really needed for aircraft engines, in which the 'lighter the better' was clearly what was required. There was also discussion between Power Jets and BTH about the inaccuracy of BTH machining, which was not much of a problem for their traditional large and heavy steam turbines, but critically important for the new lightweight jet engine designs.

At the end of the day, of course, jet engine manufacturing would be undertaken by companies such as Rolls-Royce, which had always recognised the need for high-accuracy machining for lightweight and high power-to-weight ratio aircraft engines.

An important conference was held on 12 April 1940, at the Air Ministry that would largely dictate the future of Power Jets. Air Vice-Marshal Tedder opened the meeting by saying that the Ministry had decided that BTH and Rover would share production of the new jet engines. He said that contracts for the manufacturing work would go directly to these two firms, rather than to Power Jets, which would then sub-contract to the much larger firms. He also indicated that Power Jets would be maintained as a 'research organisation', which would ultimately end Whittle's dream of seeing all design, development and production of his new engine being the purview of Power Jets. There was also disagreement at the meeting between BTH, who believed that they should be responsible for the final construction drawings, and Whittle, who realised that Power Jets was better placed for the type of fine detail work needed for the new lightweight engines. In the end, however, Tedder's view that Power Jets would focus on research and development, rather than large-scale production, would stand.

Later on Whittle expressed his dissatisfaction at having not been consulted beforehand on the Ministry's decision, but realised that it was a fait accompli. In a subsequent meeting at the Air Ministry on 10 May, Whittle held extensive discussions with Tedder and Sir Wilfred Freeman. After being told that the Ministry was expecting that BTH and Rovers would be doing the 'basic design work', with assistance from Power Jets, Whittle expressed his 'dissatisfaction that I had not been consulted on the Air Ministry's arrangements'. During the meeting he also told Tedder and Freeman that he 'had a strong dislike of Mr Whyte' and that, 'Whyte's manner and way of going about things was enough to get anybody's back up.' In a memo about the meeting, however, he wrote, 'Nevertheless I felt bound to say that if he were more acquainted with Mr Whyte's motives he would find them all he could wish them to be; that Mr Whyte always put the National interest before any other considerations.'[20] Tedder then said that 'he had made up his mind very definitely some time ago that in no circumstances would he allow a small company to be swallowed by two large ones, and that this was still his attitude in spite of severe provocation' from the larger, established companies.

This was, of course, a very critical period for Britain, as the Battle of France took place from early May until late June 1940, ending with the occupation of the whole country. Near the end of May, Whittle had a meeting with William Lawrence Tweedie, the Air Ministry Director of Engine Development, in which Tweedie mentioned that there might be a need for Power Jets to shut down due to other 'higher priorities'. With typical British understatement, he told Whittle that this might be for a period of several months as 'the country would probably be specially concentrated on immediate requirements'. Shortly after this discussion the Battle of Britain took place in the air from early July to the end of September 1940, in which the Royal Air Force faced its biggest ever challenge. Fortunately, the RAF was just able to repel the Luftwaffe, with the great bravery and skill of a relatively small group of fighter pilots and a large number of ground forces manning anti-aircraft guns. After the RAF had successfully forestalled a German invasion, Whittle was pleased to see a telegram to Whyte from Tedder in which he said that 'work should proceed under priority 1A of the Ministry of Supply'. He also learned that a proposal to move the whole development work on his engine to Canada had been turned down following the successful conclusion of the war in the air over Britain.

The next two years, 1941 and 1942, were taken up with almost continuous redesigning and testing of the engine in order to improve its reliability and increase the thrust produced. This period also marked a major expansion of the Power Jets workforce, which was now being funded almost entirely from Air Ministry contracts. The facilities at the Ladywood Works became increasingly crowded, with the shortage of office space for Whittle and his growing group of detail designers being especially acute. In mid-1940 Power Jets had leased a major portion of a small country house, Brownsover Hall (see Plate 13), which was located about halfway between the Ladywood Works in Lutterworth and Whittle's home in nearby Rugby. This lovely old house, now a small hotel, made a huge improvement in Whittle's working conditions, and enabled him to have a large office in which he could spread out working drawings and also consult with the detailed designers and draftsmen who worked in nearby rooms. Power Jets had also retained a car and driver, which facilitated the frequent shuttling of Whittle and his design staff between the Ladywood Works and Brownsover Hall. By this time Whittle also had a secretary, Ms Mary Phillips, who had begun her work in the very crowded office space in the Ladywood Works and was one of the first small group of Power Jets employees. She went with him when he moved to Brownsover Hall, and was instrumental in helping to organise the growing group working there. It was her responsibility to organise his very busy diary and to ensure that he was kept up to date with Power Jets company affairs and the increasingly large volume of official correspondence. She was devoted to Whittle, and kept in touch with him long after she had left the company.

In retrospect this period really marked the beginning of a clear path to commercial development of the jet engine, and its universal use in all but the smallest aeroplanes. As the staff of Power Jets grew, there was less call on the engineers and technicians of BTH for design and testing work. The disagreement between Whittle and BTH over turbine blade design, and Whittle's subsequent patenting of the 'vortex-flow' blade design, had also led to Power Jets renewing their search for other firms that may be interested in making components to Whittle's design. In another one of those fortuitous connections, Col Tinling's wife was a friend of the wife of Maurice Wilks, who was chief engineer of the Rover car company, while his elder brother Spencer Wilks was managing director. Spencer Wilks was married to the daughter of William Hillman and both brothers had started out working for the Hillman car company. Spencer Wilks then took over running the company when William Hillman died. After the takeover of Hillman by the Rootes group, both brothers became disillusioned by the new management and moved to Rover. Initially Spencer was the works manager at Rover, but in 1934 after the company made substantial losses a reorganisation resulted in him becoming managing director and Maurice becoming chief engineer, the position he had ultimately had at Hillman. The two Wilks brothers, who achieved automotive fame by conceiving the iconic Land Rover after the war, had by then tight control of operations at Rover, and could quickly make important decisions about the company's future.

Tinling arranged for a meeting between Whittle and Maurice Wilks in early 1940, during which Whittle described his need for help in manufacturing components for his jet engine, which was clearly becoming a commercial reality at that time. Wilks found the project intriguing, and believed Rover's expertise in complex sheet metal fabrication in particular might make a good fit with the jet engine, in which there were a large number of sheet metal components. These included the combustion chamber 'cans' as well as the complex ductwork linking the chambers to the compressor outlet and turbine inlet. He also indicated that his brother may be interested in having Rover provide some investment capital in Power Jets.

Whittle, of course, was delighted by this response, and a follow-up meeting was arranged with both Wilks brothers and a Power Jets team represented by Whittle, Tinling and Dudley-Williams. At this meeting Spencer Wilks indicated that he had heard much about the technical details of Whittle's engine, and believed that Rover could well do much of the manufacturing required for production examples. He also indicated that the company may well be interested in investing in Power Jets, thereby becoming full partners in an exciting new venture. Whittle had to explain, however, that Power Jets was now nearly wholly funded by the Air Ministry and furthermore that they had no patent position as Whittle had let his original patent lapse, and all subsequent patent rights were held by the government as Whittle was still a serving officer.

Wilks was advised that he should hold talks with senior members of the Air Ministry, who by this time were really calling all the shots at Power Jets. These included Air Vice-Marshal Tedder, now the Director General for Research; Major George Bulman, Assistant Director of Engine Development; Dr David Pye, Director of Scientific Research; and finally Sir Henry Tizard, Chairman of the Aeronautical Research Committee. Tizard had been a chemist at Oxford University before the war, and had been instrumental in wide-ranging research related to fuel quality, including development of the octane rating system for petrol, which is still used. He was widely respected and had risen through the ranks of academia in the 1930s to become the Rector (equivalent to President) of Imperial College London. During the war he was appointed as Chairman of the Aeronautical Research Committee, which had a wide-ranging overview of all new developments in research related to the war in the air. Importantly, he also had the ear of Winston Churchill, with whom he consulted on a wide range of technical issues related to the war, including aircraft production, jet engines and the development of radar. Tizard was very impressed with Whittle's abilities and his steely determination to see his jet engine concept through to successful deployment for the war effort. In 1937, not long after the formation of Power Jets, Whyte had written to Tizard to ask him for his opinion of Whittle's novel ideas for a new form of aircraft propulsion. Tizard's reply was very instructive and likely provided a huge boost for the prospects of the radical new engine design proposed by Whittle. It is worth seeing Tizard's reply in its entirety:

22nd June, 1937

Dear Mr Whyte,

You ask for my opinion about Flight Lieutenant Whittle's scheme.
    I think there is nothing inherently unsound in his ideas. He may possibly be somewhat optimistic in some of his predictions, but even allowing for that I think it highly probable that, if he has the necessary financial support and encouragement, he will succeed in producing a new type of power plant for aircraft. I am particularly interested in this work because I think that, if we are to provide the high powers which will be necessary for aircraft of the future, we must develop some type of turbine. Further, the fact that such an engine would use heavy oil is of great importance from the point of view of defence and of commerce.
    I have a very high opinion of Flight Lieutenant Whittle. He has the ability, the energy and the enthusiasm for work of this nature. He has also an intimate knowledge of practical conditions. This combination of qualities is rare and deserves the utmost encouragement. I sincerely hope you will get the

necessary finance because I think you will have to make up your mind that a large expenditure will be necessary before final success is reached. My general opinion of the importance of this work leads me to express the hope that the money will be raised privately so that the knowledge that it is going on will not be widespread.

Yours sincerely,

H.T. Tizard

P.S. Of course I do not mean to imply that success is certain. All new schemes of this kind must be regarded as a 'gamble' in the initial stages. I do think however that this is a better gamble than many I know of, on which much money has been spent!

In late January 1940 Tizard visited Power Jets to see what progress was being made by Whittle and his team. In a memorandum summarising his visit Whittle wrote that Tizard was given a successful demonstration and he appears to be acting on the statement that 'a demonstration which does not break down in my presence is a production job'. Following the demonstration, Tizard implied that he would support Power Jets' programme to gain experience with further development and ultimately manufacturing, which might follow in twelve to eighteen months' time. He also suggested that Power Jets should equip themselves to carry out tests on a single combustion chamber, since this was such a crucial component of the engine. Tizard also told Whittle that he believed the ideal fighter design of the future would be a twin-engine, two-seater aircraft. He emphasized that this would enable a second occupant to be fully engaged in locating and shooting down enemy aircraft, thus relieving the pilot to fully concentrate on flying at the very high speeds he envisaged would be made possible by the new engine design. Tizard also mentioned to Whittle before he left that the Ministry was not aware of any foreign work on jet propulsion, although there had been some vague rumours of such developments in Germany. After questioning from Whittle, Tizard also indicated that there should be no discussions with the French government or armed forces about the new propulsion system until the new design was 'in the air'. Needless to say, Whittle was very pleased with the outcome of the visit and thought that he had strong support from the Aeronautical Research Committee.

In mid-February Air Vice-Marshal Tedder also paid a visit to Power Jets to see for himself the new propulsion system that he had been hearing about. He was accompanied by David Pye, William Tweedie, the Director of Engine Development, and William Scott Farren, the Deputy Director of Scientific Research in the Air Ministry.

After a demonstration run Tedder wrote a brief note to Whittle, saying:

> Just a note to say how glad I was to have an opportunity to see your 'child' in action. It really is a fascinating and impressive job, and having seen it, I shall certainly feel more than before that it is up to me to do all I can to move it forward.

There is little doubt that, coming from someone he regarded so highly, this was very encouraging to Whittle. However, following discussions with Farren over lunch, Whittle became quite depressed about the likely future prospects for the commercial success of Power Jets. Farren was also a Cambridge man, having studied at Trinity College, graduating in 1914 with a first-class degree in the mechanical sciences tripos. During the First World War he had joined the rapidly growing Royal Aircraft Factory, and became the chief aerodynamicist. In 1920 he returned to Cambridge as a lecturer in aeronautical engineering, and then with war again looming in 1937 he joined the Air Ministry as Deputy Director of Scientific Research. His views on the commercial prospects for Power Jets, therefore, were likely to be important for the future of the company, which resulted in Whittle writing to him soon after the meeting. It is instructive to read Whittle's letter in full:

16th February 1940

W.S. Farren Esq.
Air Ministry
HARROGATE
Yorks.

Dear Mr Farren,

During our conversation at lunch time yesterday you made various remarks, some of which were to the following effect.

1. People who had put their money in Power Jets were an unselfish crowd of people who had done a very good job of work, and that there was no hope of them ever getting any return on their money, and that in fact they would be very lucky indeed if they ever made good their loss.
2. The Air Ministry would not allow Power Jets to become a manufacturing organisation and intended to keep it as a small research organisation, and that for manufacture some existing firm would be used.
3. That nobody would make anything out of this engine because it belonged wholly to the Air Ministry and the Department

would see that nobody made anything out of it. There would only be the normal legitimate manufacturing profit (from which Power Jets was excluded).
4. That the Air Ministry did not like Mr Whyte's suggestion of an organisation to handle manufacture in which Power Jets would be part owners.
5. That it is not healthy for an organisation such as ours to depend so much on Air Ministry money; that it should get private money as well, but that it was of little use anybody putting money into Power Jets because if they did so they would lose it, there being no way by which they get a normal return, Power Jets having no patent position by virtue of the fact that the Air Ministry controlled the situation in this respect, and no manufacturing rights.
6. That the Air Ministry would not place orders with Power Jets for other than experimental engines, and definitely would not place orders for other engines through Power Jets.

It is fortunate that I regard the above as expressions of your own opinion, and not those of the Department, as otherwise I would be most upset, since it would seem to me grossly unfair that the Air Ministry should allow Power Jets to ripen the fruit and others to pluck it. I am not after big dividends myself, but at the same time it would be weigh heavily on me if I thought that many individuals who had put their money in largely because of their faith in me are not to see a just return on that money in the future. In any case I regard Power Jets organisation as almost as much my creation as the engine itself, and for that reason I want to see it expand. It is in a sense my only 'command' and I believe that Power Jets as such could handle this job in the future stages better than some existing aero engine firm, who would probably rather kill it than get on with it.

We have plenty of evidence that the wolves are gathering round the door, and I have a very depressing feeling that your sympathies lie with the wolves.

I am sending a copy of this letter to Air Vice-Marshal Tedder because the above touches quite closely some of the subjects discussed in my recent meeting with him.

Yours sincerely,
F. Whittle

Tedder then sent a brief reassuring note to Whittle in which he said;

Don't worry about what Farren might have said on financial matters, which are not his concern. Neither he nor I are in a position to discuss the financial aspects of the company, either in the past or in the future. On the other hand, I dislike wolves as much as you do and you can be assured that my sympathies do not lie with them.

In retrospect it can be seen that Farren's letter did quite accurately describe the position that Power Jets, and by extension, Whittle, found themselves in. There had been a rapid expansion of the company, which had grown from five employees at the end of 1938 to twenty-five at the beginning of 1940, and then to fifty-nine by August 1940. Even so, Whittle found it very hard to accept that Power Jets was not in a position to expand to the extent needed to build the thousands of engines that would be required to make a significant contribution to the war effort. And, by virtue of the fact that all of the intellectual property rights belonged to the UK government as a result of Whittle being a serving RAF officer, there were no realistic prospects for Power Jets to become a major engine manufacturer in the middle of a war. Although Whittle must have seen this to be the case, he found it very hard to accept, and as a result he ended up suffering from severe depression on and off for several years to come.

This period also marked the turn away from BTH and to Rover for the manufacturing of jet engines, particularly various versions of the W2 production engine. It was also clear that the Air Ministry was now in full control of the future development of jet engines. On 26 March 1940, a critical meeting was held that essentially eliminated the ability of Power Jets, and therefore its key shareholders, to benefit financially from Whittle's ground-breaking invention, as had been predicted by Farren. The meeting was chaired by Air Vice-Marshal Tedder and attendees included Whittle and Whyte representing Power Jets, the Wilks brothers from Rover and several officials from the Air Ministry, including Dr Pye and a representative from the contracts division. The purpose of the meeting was to determine the future role of the various parties in bringing the jet engine into production. Tedder opened the meeting by explaining that it was the Air Ministry's intent to see that jet engines were put into production as soon as possible in order to help the war effort. He, and the other Air Ministry officials present, pointed out that the Ministry had control of all of Whittle's patent rights, and they intended to put these to use in the interest of winning the war. As a somewhat amusing aside, Whittle noted that Farren had insisted that he (Whittle) should not be allowed to fly the new Gloster prototype fighter powered by his engine design because 'it was important that I should not go up in smoke'!

Tedder indicated that the Air Ministry had decided to call in a firm with considerable production experience and suitable plant to undertake development and manufacturing of the radical new propulsion system. He indicated that it was the Ministry's intention to give orders directly to Rover and they hoped for 'a very intimate basis of cooperation between the Rover Company and Power Jets'.

Whittle was shocked to learn that it was the Ministry's intention to contract directly with Rover, and they expected that Power Jets would provide their full cooperation and provide detailed design information to that company. Spencer Wilks then asked where Power Jets came into the picture, and pointed out that they had spent a lot of private money on development to date. Wilks then said that if the Air Ministry proposed to order engines from Rovers 'he could not see what Power Jets was going to get out of it, and this seemed to be morally wrong and very unfair'.[19] Tedder then replied that the Air Ministry agreed with this in principle and there was then a discussion on what could be done for Power Jets. Wilks then suggested that perhaps Rover could pay Power Jets for a licence in which the Air Ministry would need to join. However, Mr Tweedie and Mr Pye pointed out that officially there could be no question of a licence fee because the Crown had full rights of free use. Air Ministry officials also said that there could be no question of a royalty as the designs were the property of the Ministry by contract. This discussion essentially ended any commercial prospects that Power Jets might have had, and sealed the fate of the company, which would ultimately transition into a Government research facility.

Whittle was, of course, greatly disappointed by this news, but as a serving officer he knew that his duty was to comply fully and cooperate with Rover as closely as he could. The outcome of the meeting surprised even Spencer Wilks, who said to Tedder at one point, 'It seems as if you hold all the cards,' to which Tedder answered, 'Yes, including the joker,' and pointed at Whittle.[20]

Whittle and Whyte, representing Power Jets, held another meeting with Air Ministry officials on 12 April 1940 to finalise the details of the new working relationship that had been decided by the Ministry.

Air Vice-Marshal Tedder again chaired the meeting, and opened the discussions by saying that the Ministry had decided that both BTH and Rover would share the production of jet propulsion engines. The Ministry would give direct contracts with both firms and Power Jets would be expected to give them every assistance and co-operate with both firms 'on the closest possible basis'. Tedder said that 'the key to the whole situation was Sqn. Leader Whittle, and he would be expected to co-operate fully with the engineers at both firms'.[21]

Power Jets would be maintained as a research organisation, and they would be paid an adequate sum for their research work and supply of design drawings and information. In reply to an enquiry by Whyte, Tedder said that civil rights did not enter into the matter, and Power Jets would continue to retain these. He concluded by saying that BTH and Rover, 'the two contracted manufacturing firms would have no special rights in this matter'. Although this statement seemed to give a ray of hope for the prospects of Power Jets following the war, subsequent events would prove this to be a false hope.

In his memorandum summarising his visit to the Air Ministry, Whittle wrote that, 'It became clear that the Air Ministry's interpretation of their wishes in relation to design itself went beyond our own views on the subject, and that it appeared that the Air Ministry was expecting the Rover Company and the B.T.H. to do the basic design work, with our assistance.'

Whittle then went on to tell Tedder that he believed that neither company could tackle the primary design, unless they brought in new personnel. He thought that Rover 'would not even be able to look at it but the BTH could do a large part of the preliminary design'. He also believed, however, that BTH were suffering from a severe shortage of really competent engineers, with the exception of Mr Cheshire, who was already on full-time loan to Power Jets and was participating in the design activities.

Following his discussions with Tedder, Whittle was taken to a meeting with Air Chief Marshal Sir Wilfrid Freeman, who as Vice Chief of the Air Staff was responsible for ordering most of the aircraft and related supplies for the RAF. Freeman told Whittle that he had made up his mind that that 'there was to be the strongest possible effort to make a show of the new engine'. He went on to say that, 'If he (Whittle) had any ideas that he wanted made they must be made in addition to anything else that Rover and BTH were making on their own account, and there would be no financial restrictions on the whole development whatsoever.' Whittle replied by saying that 'there was a good deal that was new to me, and encouraging'. Freeman ended the meeting by telling Whittle that he was not to hesitate to phone directly to either Tedder or himself, or go up to see them if there was any difficulty or anything else likely to cause delay.

In early June 1940, Whittle was asked by Sir Henry Tizard to give him an update on progress with the new engine. Whittle wrote a detailed letter to Tizard, in which he outlined progress to date with the experimental work, and shared some of his frustration at not making progress as quickly as he had hoped.[22] He started by telling Tizard that 'the experimental engine has not blown up yet', indicating his frustration at the slow progress being made on improving the combustion process. He then provided a detailed summary of progress to date, focusing on the ongoing problems related to obtaining stable combustion. He noted that they could achieve reasonably consistent and stable combustion in a stand-alone combustor test rig, but not in the engine itself. He then went on to describe the intention of the Air Ministry to place manufacturing contracts for the new engine directly with BTH and the Rover company, with little input from Power Jets or Whittle himself. He ended by saying that he did not share the Air Ministry's confidence that the two large companies had the ability to do all of the necessary design work on their own. He clearly indicated his frustration at being sidelined, saying that 'in other words my position as chief engineer on the job has been seriously weakened, and I do not like it much. However, I will do my best in the joint effort.'

As Whittle's revolutionary new engine became ever closer to production reality, news of his accomplishments began to reach into the highest echelons of the government, and the Air Ministry in particular. As a result, on 9 July 1940, Whittle was summoned to a meeting at the recently established Ministry of Aircraft Production (or MAP as it was universally known), headed by the indomitable Canadian press baron Lord Beaverbrook. Beaverbrook, a larger than life individual and very close confidant of Churchill, had a well-deserved reputation for not suffering fools, and for always getting immediately to the heart of any problem, no matter how insoluble it may seem to mere mortals. It's likely that it was these very qualities that led Churchill to appoint him as Minister of Aircraft Production, arguably the most important ministry during this stage of the war.

Whittle's meeting with Beaverbrook was brief, but was very likely instrumental in ensuring that subsequent development of the revolutionary new engine was not hindered by lack of resources from the MAP. After a brief introduction to the engine by Whittle, Beaverbrook asked him if he had seen Air Vice-Marshal Hill, who was Director of Research and Development at the MAP. Whittle replied that he had not yet seen Hill, but that Air Vice-Marshal Tedder had been very supportive. Beaverbrook had clearly been briefed on recent development towards large-scale production of Whittle's engine, and asked if Rover and BTH were doing a satisfactory job. In his subsequent notes of the meeting Whittle noted that he had been as 'non-committal as I could make it, saying that the arrangements made by the Air Ministry were so recent that there was not yet time to judge'. The meeting ended with Beaverbrook asking when the prototype aircraft designed for the new engine would be ready. When Whittle said that it looked like being at least eighteen months away, Beaverbrook replied by saying, 'When you are ready for the prototype let me know and you shall have it.'[23]

In late August 1940, Tedder visited Power Jets and spent considerable time with Whittle discussing collaboration between Rover, BTH and Whittle's team. Immediately following these discussions he wrote to Whyte and to the chief executives of both BTH and Rover in order to clarify the working relationship between the three main parties now working on jet engine development.[24] He indicated that both BTH and Rover would be responsible for building copies of three different versions of Whittle's new engine, namely the W2A, W2B, and W2C, all of which had been designed by him and his small team. He also said that the two large manufacturing firms were to be in close contact with each other and receive 'all information they require from Power Jets Ltd'. He went on to say that the two firms would be expected to make 'the maximum possible use of the advice which Wing Commander Whittle could provide to them'. Needless to say, this was a clear blow to the dreams that Whittle, and the Power Jets team, had of becoming an independent manufacturer of his radical new concept for aircraft propulsion. For Whittle this really marked a major turning point, and he began to realise that he had essentially lost control of the commercial development of the engine he had invented and worked so hard to develop into a practical propulsion system.

Despite the positive meeting with Beaverbrook, and the reassurances from Tedder that he would not allow a small company to be swallowed up by much bigger ones, the end result of this series of meetings, and the latest letter from Tedder, was very depressing for both Whittle and Whyte. They began to see that Whittle's dream of revolutionising air travel had been handed to others for free. Whittle wrote a series of memoranda describing the many discussions he was now having with D.G. Tobin, an assistant to Dr Harold Roxbee Cox, who had been appointed as the main contact for Whittle within the Air Ministry. Whittle came to have a very high regard for Cox, who had a background much like his own, starting out as an aircraft apprentice at the age of 16 and eventually earning a PhD from Imperial College in London. He was involved in the early design of the R101 airship and then joined the Royal Aircraft Establishment to work on aircraft design. Upon the outbreak of war in 1939 Cox was transferred to the Ministry of Aircraft Production, where he became the Deputy Director of Scientific Research. In a discussion with Tobin in London on 3 September 1940, Whittle learned that both Rover and BTH had agreed to work together in producing engines to Whittle's design, and were expected to 'consult' with Whittle in order to expedite the detailed design and manufacturing of prototype engines.[25] Whittle told Tobin that he 'strongly disagreed with the Air Ministry policy', and believed that they were wasting a lot of money by involving three different firms in the development of a production-ready engine. Whittle went on to say that he 'felt so strongly about this matter that I proposed to place it on record that what the Air Ministry was doing was in the face of my advice and I wished to be dissociated from it'. He concluded by saying that the Ministry had 'lost the most precious thing in the whole business, and that was my interest'.

Another great stress on Whittle at this time was his disagreement with Lancelot Whyte, chairman of Power Jets, who had a rather abrasive personality and was not leading the company in the direction that Whittle felt was appropriate. Whyte was evidently not representing the company to the Air Ministry and the two collaborating companies, BTH and Rovers, in the way that Whittle expected. In particular, Whittle believed that Whyte had too often been misleading when relating his interactions with the Air Ministry and the other two companies to Whittle.

In a memorandum summing up his meeting with Whyte on 4 September 1940, Whittle described their most recent quarrel.[26]

He noted that 'in handling the affairs of the company, particularly in negotiation with other parties, his manner and personality were very harmful'. Whittle also said that Whyte was 'extremely tactless and was apt to make empty threats'. He also thought that Whyte's salary was far too high, and noted that this had also been mentioned to him by senior Air Ministry staff.

As the controlling shareholder in Power Jets, Whittle had the power to fire Whyte, and he asked for his resignation. However, Whittle's original partners in Power Jets, Dudley-Williams, Tinling and Bonham-Carter, had reservations about firing Whyte at such a critical time in the company's development. They even hinted to Whittle that perhaps he was being too harsh on Whyte due to the considerable stress and fatigue that he had been under for some time in trying to prove that his engine would be a success. In Whittle's notes of the resignation he said 'it appeared that they had also agreed among themselves that my dislike of Mr Whyte was quite abnormal and extreme, that I was overwrought and in need of a holiday, and generally that the time for my action has been very ill-chosen'.

Whittle had a brief conversation with Bonham-Carter, who said that he thought that AVM Tedder would put him on leave. In response, Whittle told Bonham-Carter that he did not propose to change his mind about Whyte, and said, 'I was not overwrought, and my action had been very well considered.'[27] In the event, Whittle failed to formally oust Whyte from the company.

Two days later Whittle spoke to Tedder, who had requested a meeting following his discussions with Bonham-Carter and Whyte. As predicted by Bonham-Carter, Tedder opened the conversation by asking Whittle if he would like to go on a 'refresher' flying training course.[28] Whittle indicated that although he would like to go on a training course, he was in the middle of moving house, and felt that he couldn't immediately go flying. Tedder then went on to ask Whittle what he thought of a proposal from the Air Ministry to have an arbitration session following the end of the war in order to sort out the commercial positions of Power Jets, Rover and BTH related to their work on the new engine. Whittle replied that he hadn't thought about that, and wasn't going to worry about the commercial position of the three firms.

Tedder then went on to say that both Sporborg of BTH and Wilks of Rover had serious misgivings about Whyte's role in controlling the development of the new engine. Whittle said that he knew that to be the case, and that he was also concerned about Whyte's serious lack of tact in dealing with others who were likely looking forward to commercial development of the engine following the war. Tedder then said that he didn't have the power to stop Whittle from removing Whyte from his position at Power Jets, and would leave it to Whittle to sort out. He also said he believed that Whittle should be free to drive the technical direction of development, but that the engineer in charge shouldn't be burdened by concerning himself with the commercial matters. Tedder ended the meeting by saying that he thought that the companies who would be building engines in large quantities should be free to do some development work. Whittle no doubt felt quite distressed at the way in which Tedder clearly believed that companies much larger than Power Jets would ultimately be the ones to fully commercialise his ingenious new powerplant.

On 18 October 1940, Air Chief Marshal Sir Wilfred Freeman visited Power Jets to see for himself how the new engine concept was progressing. During the discussions Whyte strongly recommended that Whittle should be put in overall charge of all engine development, including that being done by both Rover and BTH. However, Sir Wilfred declined to accept this, reinforcing Tedder's view that it 'would be distasteful to both companies'.[29] When Whittle complained about the very low standards of manufacturing in both companies, Freeman responded by saying that both companies had been 'hit very hard financially' by their war activities. He also suggested to Whittle that he should visit Rover several times a week and take much more interest in their work. Whyte then responded that expecting Whittle to teach Rover how to build the new engine would put too heavy a burden on him.

Following these meetings with senior Air Ministry personnel there appeared to be little change in the Ministry's attitude to production design and development of the new engine. It seemed to Whittle that both BTH and Rover were being allowed to work freely on their own designs, and were taking little interest in Whittle's concerns about their lack of fundamental understanding of his novel new engine design. Progress at both companies seemed to be very slow, and Whittle believed that neither was taking advantage of the technical knowledge that they could easily obtain from him and his team at Power Jets.

This time really marked a 'changing of the guard' at Power Jets, and cleared the way for the two major firms, BTH and Rover, to become the primary manufacturers of the new engine. Power Jets would retain the role of design and development, but would not become a major manufacturer. By this time Power Jets had grown to a team of some seventy-five people, putting additional strain on Whittle, who was still the 'go-to' person to answer the increasingly complex design and development questions that continued to be raised by the growing staff and the two manufacturing firms.

This period also marked the beginning of plans for large-scale manufacturing of the new jet engine by both BTH and Rover. Neither were already engaged in large-scale production for the war effort, unlike most other large companies such as Rolls-Royce. In October 1940, Rovers submitted a production plan to the Air Ministry suggesting that they could manufacture fifty of the new engines per week.

During this time, when large-scale manufacturing was being very actively discussed, Whittle attempted to ensure that Power

Jets would maintain a decisive role in producing his new designs. He wrote to Professor Lindemann, who he knew would be briefing Churchill, suggesting that he and Power Jets should have sole control of all design and development of his new engine. Shortly after this, Tedder wrote to Whittle saying that he 'would try' to ensure that all engines being built would adhere strictly to Power Jets' designs. In a letter to Power Jets, Air Vice-Marshal Tedder indicated that full design responsibility should be the sole responsibility of Power Jets. In his notes, however, Whittle suggested that these instructions were never followed and they were 'resisted' by the two larger companies. Shortly after this, however, Tedder was 'posted' to a new position, strengthening the hand of BTH and Rover to take on more design responsibility.

In November 1940, Power Jets was visited by Harry (later Sir Harry) Ricardo, who was a very well-known engineering consultant to the automotive engine companies. He was able to give some good advice on combustion to Whittle, although he later remarked to Dr William Hawthorne, seconded to Power Jets from the Royal Aircraft Establishment, that he thought it would be 'difficult to teach Power Jets much'. One of his suggestions, however, was to use fuels with a high 'Cetane number', which would prove to be beneficial in improving ignitability of the fuel-air mixture. He was also quite critical of the idea of using a 'committee' to oversee development of the jet engine, evidently a reference to a letter from Tedder in which he suggested setting up what later became the Gas Turbine Co-operation Committee.

Whittle remained supportive of Tedder, however, when he was posted to another position. He said, 'I believe that Tedder's posting was a most unfortunate thing for Power Jets and myself, because it happened at a time when he seemed to be on the point of recognising that there was a good deal of weight in the arguments I had consistently put forward, and acted accordingly.'[30]

Towards the end of November Whittle also hosted a number of visitors from large manufacturing companies who the MAP thought might be suitable for large-scale production of the new engine. One of these visits was the automobile manufacturer Vauxhall, but Whittle was rather dismissive, suggesting that they were used to 'heavy work' and had no experience with light alloys.

Another visitor to Power Jets that month was Tobin, who suggested that Sporborg at BTH was 'intensely hostile' to Power Jets, which only seemed to confirm Whittle's opinion about the unsuitability of the company to manufacture his engine. Now that large-scale manufacturing seemed more likely than ever, both BTH and Rover were increasingly concerned with the interest being taken by other firms. Rover, in particular, seemed to be worried about Vauxhall, at the time a much larger automotive firm. Spencer Wilks of Rover even suggested that 'they would be handing the drawings straight over to Germany', which seemed unlikely.

In a further blow to Whittle, he had received a letter from the Air Ministry in late October concerning his request to file foreign patent applications. Although he was given permission to file for patents in the US, Australia and Canada, the letter went on to say that 'the permission granted herein does not in any way imply that commercial rights will be granted to you in respect of any of the inventions'.[31] As a result of this letter, the depressing series of meetings with the Air Ministry, and the challenges of working with Whyte and the growing team at Power Jets, Whittle began to have a series of health crises. From 1 to 11 January 1941 he was hospitalised for the first of what would become several 'nervous breakdowns', as mental fatigue was usually described at the time. This was no doubt due to Whittle's realisation that full commercial development of his radical new aircraft propulsion system had effectively been handed to Rover, who would benefit from all the dedication and hard work from his team at Power Jets.

In early 1941, Hawthorne visited Rover and was surprised to see their plans for redesigning the engine. When Hawthorne, who much later would become Head of the Engineering Department at Cambridge University and Master of Churchill College, reported this to Whittle it only confirmed his worst fears and increased his despair.

Shortly after leaving hospital, Whittle visited Tizard in London, who suggested that Vauxhall's would 'drop out' of production plans for the new engines, as they were busy building tanks for the war effort.

Tizard suggested that it was 'now or never' for large-scale production to begin, and convened a meeting at BTH with Rover and Vauxhall executives, as well as representatives from Power Jets. Plans were then drawn up to use Rover's No. 2 Shadow Factory in Coventry, in which 2,000 engines per year could be constructed. To support this, Tobin told the Wilks brothers that the new jet was to have priority over the tank engines they had been making. The term shadow factory was used at the time to indicate that war-related manufacturing would be carried out alongside, or in the 'shadow', of the pre-war automotive production that was still being undertaken there. It was also agreed that Rover should be given a contract to produce W2 engines, as soon as the Rover-developed version of Whittle's engine proved satisfactory during early testing.

At the end of January 1941, Hawthorne was pleased to receive a letter from Isaac Lubbock of Shell, confirming that he believed Power Jets had 'solved the combustion problem'.

Although Whittle was clearly pleased with these developments, he had concerns about the independent developments now going on at BTH. On 28 January, during a visit to Lutterworth by a number of visitors from the Air Ministry including Roxbee Cox, Bulman – the Assistant Director of Engine Development – and Tobin, he suggested that the work being undertaken by BTH on their own version of the engine should be stopped because it was interfering with the work they were doing for Power Jets. In response, Roxbee Cox suggested that Whittle should provide a list of everything he wanted BTH to manufacture in the future. Although this was positive news to Whittle, it did not really address the issue of BTH's independent work on their version of the W2B engine.

Bulman had opened the meeting by saying that he had 'completely changed his opinion of the whole venture in the last few days'.[32] He went on to say that he had been 'very sceptical about the whole project but that Power Jets had made some remarkable advances recently which had quite changed his outlook and he proposed to take a close interest in it in the future'.

Over lunch at the nearby Denbigh Arms hotel the group was joined by Whyte, who asked the Ministry staff for permission to order more of the special K-42-B alloy material from the US in order to manufacture more rotors. This, at the time exotic, titanium alloy had been developed by Westinghouse and had the strength of stainless steel, but weighed only about 60 per cent of the steel equivalent, making it ideal for highly stressed aircraft engine parts. Whittle was also able to get agreement from the Air Ministry staff that Power Jets should remain as the primary engine testing facility, leaving the other firms to concentrate on volume production. This informal agreement would be challenged in the future, however, as the much larger firms increasingly began design work on their own versions of Whittle's engine.

Following lunch, the Air Ministry staff and Whittle drove to the Power Jets design office in Brownsover Hall, some 6 miles away from the research facilities at Lutterworth. Waiting for the group there was Maurice Wilks, technical director of Rover, who were now fully engaged in manufacturing three complete W2 engines to Whittle's design. They were just about at the stage where the first engine would be ready for testing, and Wilks proposed that they should now build their own test facilities. Whittle was clearly not happy with this prospect, as he believed it would ultimately open the door to Rover having full design, test and manufacturing authority over Whittle's basic concept. This led to some tension between Wilks and Whittle, with Major Bulman stepping in to rule that Rover should send their first two complete W2 engines to Power Jets to be tested. Wilks was clearly not happy with this proposal, although it was left up in the air whether Rover would be allowed to keep the third engine they were manufacturing and also build new test facilities to test this engine and perhaps future versions as well. Whittle was also unhappy with the outcome of the meeting, but it was clear that the Air Ministry were really now in the driving seat in determining the future of both the design and development of the engine.

The minutes of the meeting at Lutterworth recorded that the MAP had decided twelve two-engine fighters (to be called the Meteor) would be ordered from the Gloster Aircraft Company and would be powered by Whittle's W2B engines produced by Rover. This would end up being one of the most successful fighters ever made, with ultimately nearly 4,000 being produced in several updated iterations. The Meteor would be in front-line service with the RAF from early 1943 until 1955, and into the early 1960s with several other countries.

Chapter 6

Flight of the First Jet

Progress with engine development by Whittle and his team by early 1939 had been quite rapid, and during a visit to Power Jets at the end of June Dr Pye, the Director of Scientific Research in the Air Ministry, witnessed the engine running steadily at 16,000 rpm. He was very impressed by this demonstration and convinced the Ministry that there was indeed a future for jet propulsion. The Ministry then realised that they would need to have an aeroplane designed specifically to test the new engine and began to canvas aircraft manufacturers, all of whom were very busy building conventionally powered fighters and bombers. However, in mid-1939 they placed an order with the Gloster Aircraft Company, near Gloucester in south-west England, for an experimental single-engine aeroplane about the size of the fighter planes of the time. It was to be especially designed for installation of the jet, which was being developed by Power Jets as a flight-approved version of the original WU engine.

At the same time the Air Ministry gave an order to Power Jets for three engines designed to be suitable for flight, and these were designated the W1 family by the company. The W1X was used as an experimental unit, the W1 was the first engine approved for flight, and the W1A was used for further testing and development.

George Carter, Gloster chief designer, worked closely with Whittle to set out the specifications and detailed design of the aeroplane prototype, which is now displayed in the Science Museum in London. The design produced by Glosters was a simple low-wing, single-seat monoplane designated E.28/39. This somewhat unusual designation was simply due to the standard Air Ministry practice of denoting that this was the twenty-eighth experimental specification issued in 1939. By today's standards it was a small aeroplane, having a length of just under 9m and a wing area of 14sqm. The all-up weight was 1,700kg and the fuel capacity was 81 gallons, or 370 litres. In other words, it wasn't much bigger than a large-sized car. The engine specification was for a take-off thrust of 860lb, or 3.8kN. A little over a year after the specifications were finally agreed, and following a frenzy of detailed design and development, the E.28/39 was ready for flight in early April 1941.

In order to facilitate engine installation and taxiing trials, Power Jets had shipped the W1X experimental engine to Glosters in early 1941. A small team of Power Jets employees travelled from Lutterworth down to Gloucester to help with the trial installation. In the meantime, the very experienced Gloster chief test pilot, Gerry Sayer, had been briefed on the aeroplane, and on what he might expect from the behaviour of the unusual engine located in the mid-section of the fuselage with an elongated exhaust duct leading to the tail. As an ex-RAF pilot himself, he had known Whittle for several years, and had recently visited Power Jets in order to see the experimental engine running and to be briefed by Whittle.

The engine installation was completed in early April, and on the 7th, Whittle went down to Gloucester to witness taxiing trials at Gloster's airfield. In the late afternoon, with the engine throttle control deliberately restricted from reaching full-throttle conditions, Sayer made several runs down the runway just to get the feel of the engine and the aeroplane's handling on the ground. On each run he would open the engine throttle a little further in order to see how the engine responded and to get a feel for the effect of increasing engine speed. At the end of the day, as he debriefed the small team of Gloster and Power Jets employees, Whittle got the impression that Sayer believed there would not be enough thrust at maximum rpm to enable a successful take-off. Whittle and the Power Jets team were not concerned by this, however, as they knew that the engine thrust varied in a highly non-linear manner during opening of the throttle, reaching its maximum value rather abruptly just towards the final position.[33]

The next morning, and with the full knowledge that the W1X engine had been used heavily for testing and was not cleared for flight, the Power Jets team nevertheless removed all restrictions on throttle movement. Although Whittle had been told not to try flying the aeroplane himself, he could not resist getting into the cockpit and performing some taxi trials. He did several runs down the short runway, with increased throttle opening each time, but not quite daring to open it all the way. It was, however, very satisfying to him that after all the uncertainty and difficulties in bringing his novel engine form to life he was finally able to have the thrill of being propelled down the runway by jet thrust. Whittle had never doubted the outcome of all the hard work put in by his Power Jets team and their colleagues at BTH and the other contractors. It was, however, very satisfying to see how close his 'baby' was to becoming the new standard of aviation propulsion.

After lunch on the next day, 8 April, Sayer again took the controls and made a series of excursions down the runway, each time with a slight increase in throttle. And, despite knowing that the W1X engine was officially 'un-airworthy' he could not resist pushing on until near the end of the day the little aeroplane briefly left the runway on several of his last test runs. In each case there was just a little 'hop', lasting no more than a few hundred metres, but he nevertheless felt it to be exhilarating. From then on he had no doubt that the E.28/39, with a proper flight-approved version of the W1 engine, would provide a clear demonstration of the capability of this radical new form of propulsion system.

Both Sayer and Whittle were impressed by how smooth the engine was during the taxiing trials, and how quiet it was in the cockpit compared to a conventionally powered fighter. Of course, this was mainly due to the lack of a very loud piston engine, which would normally be located ahead of the pilot, and to the high-speed jet exhausting right at the back of the aeroplane. After this clear demonstration of the ability of the Whittle engine to provide all the power needed for flight, the aeroplane was shipped by road to RAF Cranwell. This was in part due to the fact that the main runway there was significantly longer than the one at Gloster's airfield. In addition, however, Cranwell was a much more remote location than the airfield on the outskirts of Gloucester. It was also thought by all concerned that it would be much better to have the actual flight trials well away from where they could be readily observed by civilians. In the climate of wartime secrecy this could have led to very awkward questions being asked about this new and very strange form of aircraft that seemed to fly without a propeller.

At Cranwell, the well-used W1X was removed and replaced by the W1, which had been completed after the W1X by the team at Power Jets using components made by BTH and other suppliers. This engine had also now completed twenty-five hours of running time at Lutterworth without incident, which enabled it to be certified as a 'flight engine'. It was then shipped to Cranwell for installation in the E.28/39 in early May.

On 15 May, Sayer was on hand at Cranwell, and the time had finally arrived to attempt a take-off in the little jet engined Gloster aeroplane. The weather at the start of the day was typical of that in British springtime, rather cloudy and blustery and not at all suitable for test flying. Later in the day, however, the weather cleared up, and with a small crowd watching, including Whittle, Sayer prepared to take-off at 7.30pm. Without any fanfare, he taxied out to the end of the runway, and after opening up the throttle he hurtled down the runway, lifting off after a run of only about 600m. Once airborne, he raised the retractable undercarriage and then climbed to an altitude of 1,000ft before doing several circuits around the Cranwell airfield. The small group watching were impressed by the easy lift-off and the way in which the little aeroplane climbed so quickly without drama and with only a slight roar from the jet pipe rather than the usual deafening sounds that emanated from the usual piston-engined aeroplanes. After a total flying time of some seventeen minutes, Sayer brought the aeroplane back down neatly and made a perfect landing, almost as if he had been flying this machine for months.

In some ways, given the very small group on hand to watch the first flight, the first flight was a bit of an anticlimax. There was great joy, of course, and perhaps a considerable degree of relief among all of those watching who had been so intimately involved in getting to this stage. Whittle later recalled that someone, perhaps his old friend and patent agent Johnson, had slapped him on the back and said, 'Frank, it flies!' Whittle's immediate response to this was, 'Well, that's what it was bloody well designed to do, wasn't it?'[34]

There were no official photographers or film-makers present, and no press present to document the event. There was a small celebration that evening in the officers' mess at RAF Cranwell, of course, but other than that the whole affair was a rather low-key event. Flight trials went on for the next two weeks following the initial flight, and the little E.28/39 and the W1 engine performed without drama. Over the next two weeks Sayer completed a total of seventeen flights and ten hours of flying time, which had been the maximum specified for the brand-new propulsion system. In his summary of the testing he reported that the performance of the E.28/39 was 'better than estimated', both in speed and rate of climb. The maximum speed of 366mph (590km/h) was also much higher than expected and equal to the fastest Spitfire then in service.

Whittle was, of course, quite disappointed that he had not been allowed by his RAF superiors to be the first pilot to fly an aeroplane powered by his radical new engine. This was understandable, however, as the RAF knew that successful development and implementation of the jet engine still depended very heavily on his input. At the same time they, and Whittle, were very well aware of the large risk that was always taken by a test pilot when flying a new aeroplane for the very first time. This became all too evident just eighteen months later when Sayer was testing a new gunsight system in a Hawker Typhoon at RAF Acklington, in Northumberland. The testing required him to fly out over the North Sea in order to fire harmlessly into the water far away from any populated regions. He took off but sadly never returned. A second Typhoon, piloted by Paul Dobie of the RAF Volunteer Reserve, was being flown at the same time in the tests, and it did not return to base either, leading to speculation that the two aircraft had collided.[35]

Just two days after the historic first flight of the E.28/39, Sir Henry Tizard arrived at Cranwell to meet Whittle. In hindsight, Tizard's visit over the next two days would prove to be critical for the future role of Power Jets, and Whittle himself, in commercialising jet-powered flight.[38] Upon arrival Sir Henry was able to witness the new engine in action for the first time, as the E.28/39 was in the air on its sixth test flight. In the evening he spent time in private discussions with Whyte. The next day he witnessed the E.28/39 taking off, and then travelled with Whittle, Whyte and Tobin to Lutterworth for detailed discussions on the future role of Power Jets and the sub-contractors who were now taking an increasing role in building the novel new engine.

He initially held discussions with Whyte alone, and then again with Whittle over lunch. He indicated to Whittle that much more money would have to be spent on developing large-scale production of the engine. He also said that it would seem to be unfair if Power

Jets was to remain in complete control of the new engine if taxpayers were contributing most of the financing. Tizard said that he thought there were two alternatives open for commercialisation of the new engine. The first possibility would involve the government taking over Power Jets and making it a government research agency, somewhat like the Royal Aircraft Establishment. He then suggested that the second possibility would be for Power Jets to remain as a production company, but with the government having a controlling interest. He also indicated that he was 'strongly in favour' of the second proposal. In his summary of the meeting Whittle noted that Sir Henry had assured him that the original Power Jets shareholders would receive fair treatment, and might be bought out by the government. In his notes Whittle said that he told Tizard that the government-controlled company was 'exactly such a concern that I had visualized for some time'. He also noted that Tizard seemed pleased with his own views, and asked him to 'press it home to the Power Jets side.'

During their meeting Tizard also told Whittle that the US government were 'aware' of the new engine developments, but had not received any details. They had also asked for further information, but Tizard told them that this would be premature. He also told them, however, that 'the new development was such that there was a big future for it'. Whittle then told Tizard that he thought that a small nucleus of Power Jets employees should be sent to the US, with a view to opening a branch there. Somewhat ironically, he also suggested that Whyte might be sent to run it with one or two other key employees. He told Sir Henry that Whyte might be able to do a good job in the US in view of his 'American connections'. In hindsight this seems likely to have been a slightly veiled attempt by Whittle to solve the difficulties he was having with Whyte.

As an aside, it is also interesting to note that in the detailed memo on file that Whittle wrote following this visit, as well as in most other communications at the time, he referred to the new engine throughout as a 'Gyrone', evidently in case his notes were to find their way into enemy hands.

Although Whittle was, of course, very relieved and pleased with the results of the flight trials, his mind was now fully focused on looking ahead to completion of the latest version of the Whittle engine, known as the W2B/23, even though this was being manufactured by Rover at its Barnoldswick plant. This engine, capable of producing 1,250lb of thrust, had been developed from the W1 to power the Meteor. Two days after Tizard's visit, Whittle returned to Cranwell to meet with Spencer Wilks, the managing director of Rover, who had also come to witness the flight of the jet-propelled E.28/39 along with several other visitors, including senior RAF officers and representatives from the Ministry of Aircraft Production. During their meeting Wilks suggested to Whittle that Rover needed many more machine tools to speed up engine manufacturing, while Whittle noted after the meeting that 'I refrained from saying what was on my mind, namely that it was Power Jets which ought to have all these facilities, and not the Rover Company.'[39]

In mid-June 1941, Whittle went to Derby to meet Ernest Hives, the managing director of Rolls-Royce, which had been doing sub-contract work for Rover to help with their development of Whittle's engine. Given the subsequent evolution of Rolls-Royce as one of the dominant jet engine manufacturers, it is interesting to learn that Hives was initially not terribly impressed with the concept of jet propulsion. In his notes of the meeting Whittle said, 'Mr. Hives stated frankly that though they knew of our work they had not taken it very seriously until they were informed of the flight tests and now admitted that we had made them sit up and take notice. They had heard that we were in urgent need of help, especially on the manufacturing side, and had assured the MAP that they would do what they could.

'In the case of Rovers they had promised to be "good soldiers" and make parts exactly to the Rover drawings, but they wanted to

Sir Frank Whittle, with post-graduate students at the Whittle Laboratory, Cambridge, 25 May 1973. Author, second from left.

Frank Whittle family tree.

Above: Frank Whittle's birthplace, 72 Newcombe Road, Earlsdon, Coventry.

Below: Whittle as an air mechanic apprentice.

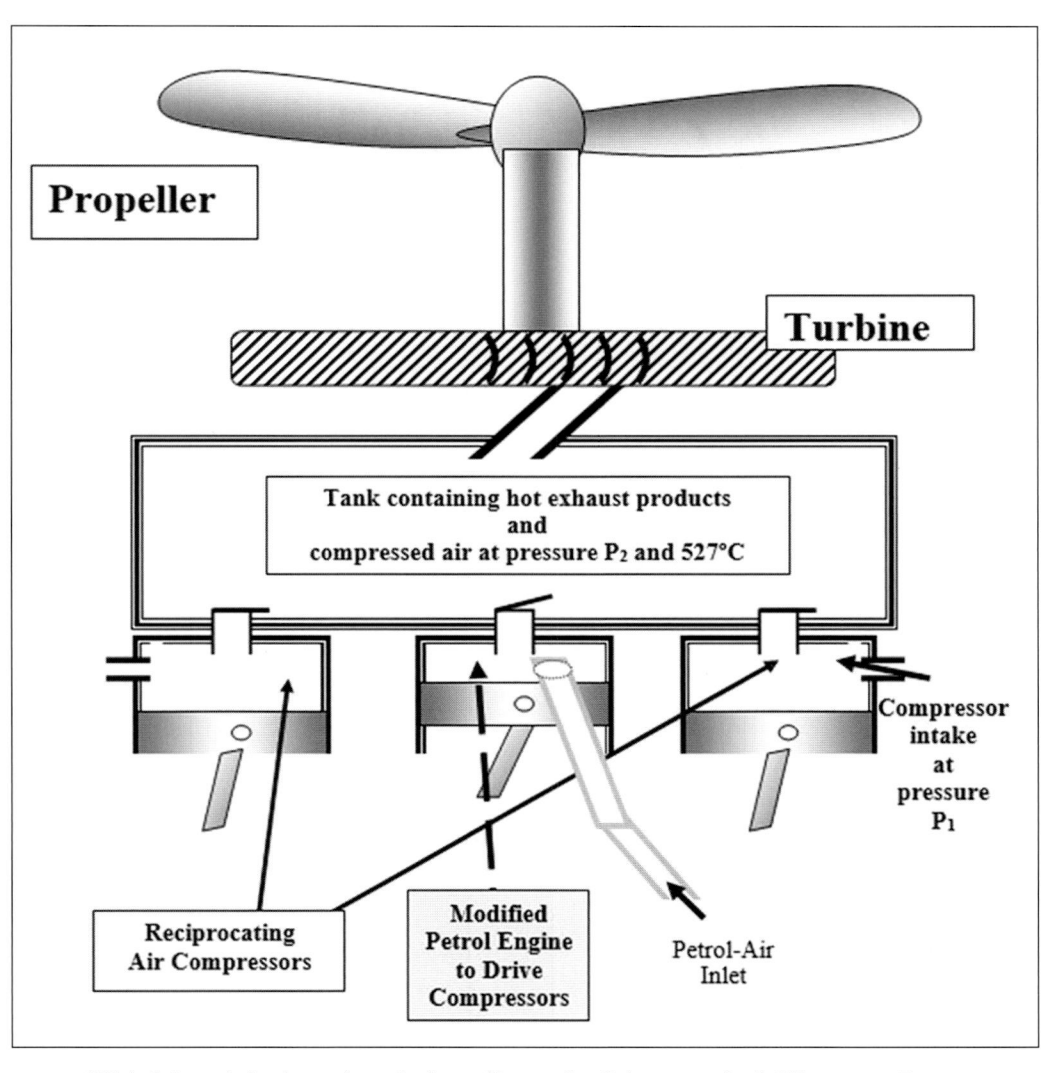

Whittle's original engine design. (Journal of Aeronautical History – Paper No. 2019/01)

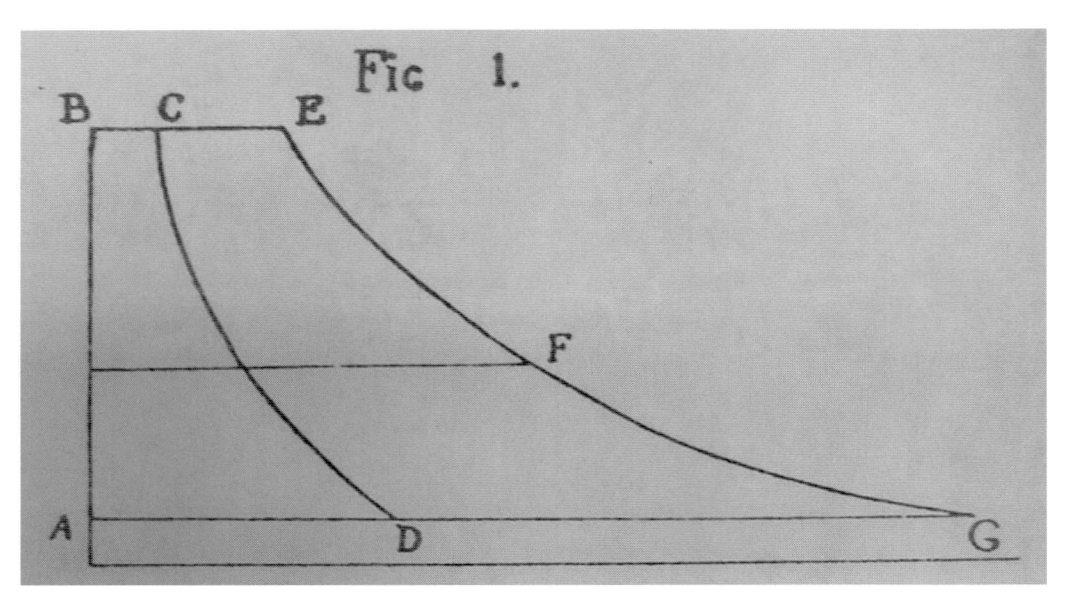

Above and below: UK Patent # 347,206, 16 April 1931.

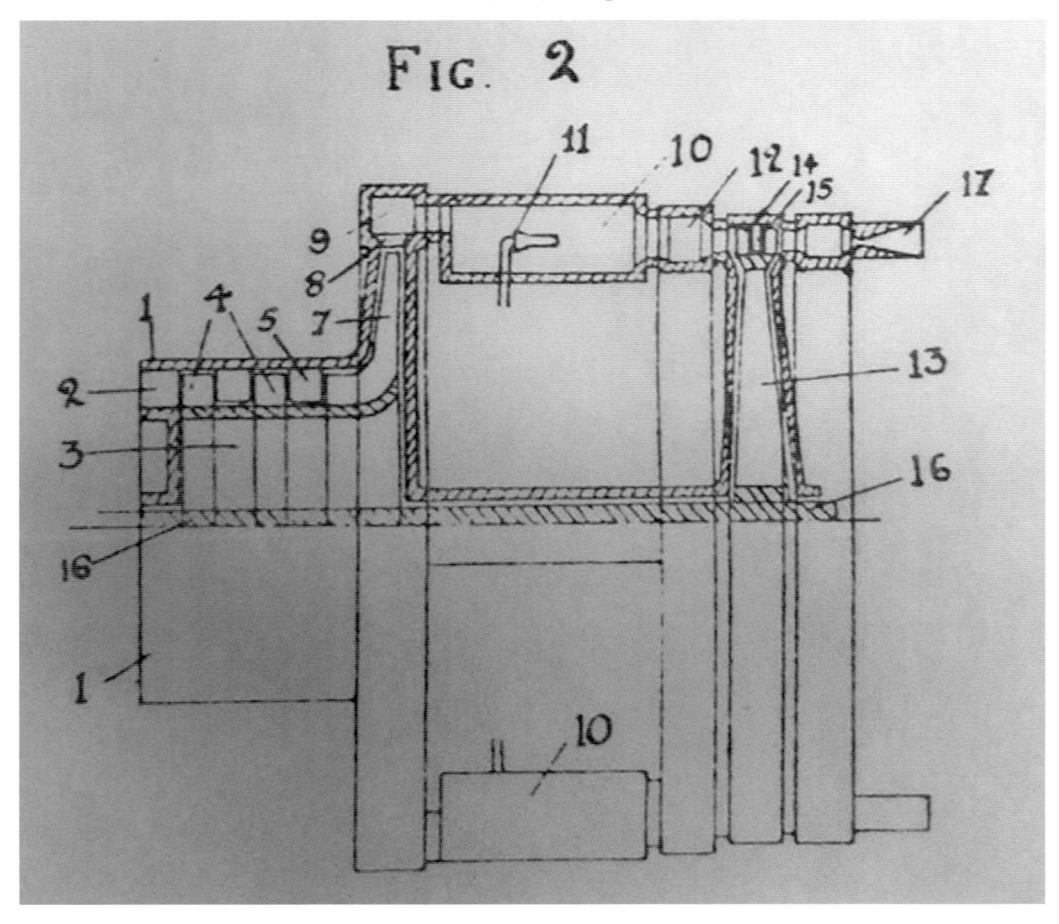

Right: Whittle all at sea, 1932.

Below: BTH–Power Jets team. (BTH Reminiscences: Sixty Years of Progress)

Air Commodore Frank Whittle

1 F. Samuelson	E	10 R. F. Loader	W
2 R. H. Collingham	E	11 J. W. Johnson	E
3 W. B. Parker	M	12 R. R. Huitson	E
4 W. A. Randles	E	13 L. Wigley	W
5 E. R. Atkinson	D	14 L. J. Cheshire	E
6 J. Richardson	D	15 W. Smith	W
7 E. H. Blade	E	16 S. A. Couling	E
8 E. Emmett	D	17 P. D. Morris	E
9 J. H. Berry	W	18 C. H. Bentley, snr.	W
19 W. A. Bailey	W		

E = Design Engineer   D = Draughtsman   W = Works Staff
M = Consulting Chemist and Metallurgist

The Ladywood Works in 2011.

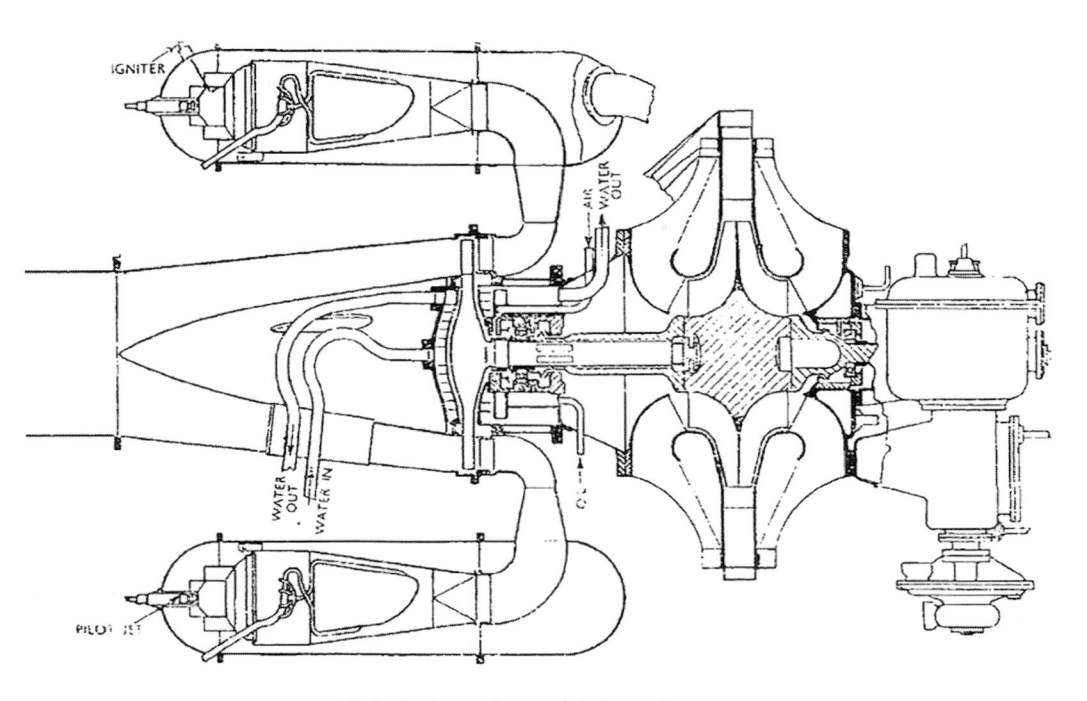

Above and below: Whittle WU engine – third version.

Brownsover Hall, near Rugby.

Above: Gloster E.28/39 first flight, 15 May 1941.

Below: W2B-500 Engine produced by Rover in 1942.

Above: Press announcement, 7 January 1944.

Left: Sir Frank Whittle. (National Portrait Gallery, NPG x99798)

Right: Whittle with Dorothy, David and Ian, 1950. (National Portrait Gallery, NPG x194393)

Below: Walland Hill in Devon.

Left: The Whittle Arches, Coventry.

Below: Rolls-Royce RB/26 Derwent.

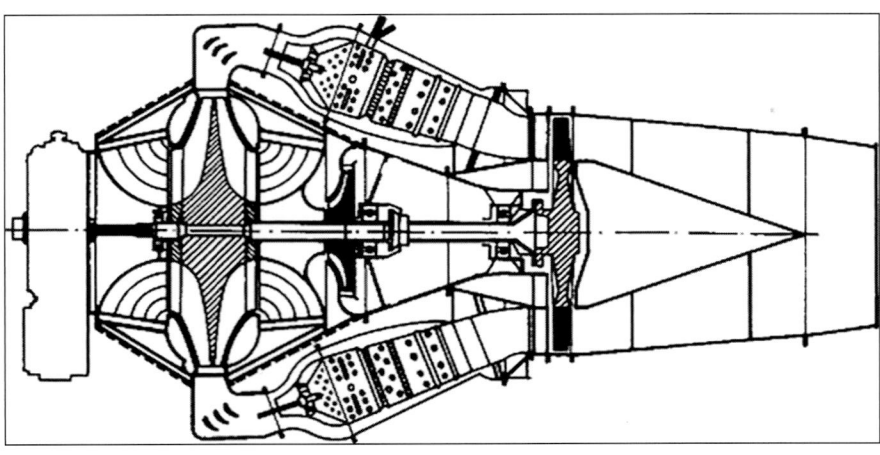

PATENT SPECIFICATION

Application Date: Jan. 16, 1930. No: 1521/30.

347,206

Complete Left: Oct 16, 1930.

Complete Accepted: April 16, 1931.

PROVISIONAL SPECIFICATION.

Improvements relating to the Propulsion of Aircraft and other Vehicles.

I, FRANK WHITTLE, of Glenhaven, Regent St., Coventry, British Subject, do hereby declare the nature of this invention to be as follows:—

This invention concerns improvements relating to propulsion and whilst at present it is deemed to be particularly adapted to the propulsion of aircraft, it is not necessarily limited to this use and may be adapted for the propulsion of other vehicles.

The main object of this invention is to provide means whereby the principle of obtaining propulsive force in the one sense of direction by the reaction caused by expelling fluid in the opposite sense of direction, may be applied efficiently to aircraft or other vehicles.

It is believed that an embodiment of this invention will provide a large thrust in proportion to its weight, that it will perform at greater altitudes than are at present obtainable, that it makes possible higher speeds than have up to the present been obtained, that it will operate with any fuel now in use, and that it will have a reasonably low fuel consumption. Further that simplicity and convenient external form is achieved.

According to the invention, a heat cycle is employed, consisting of one, or more stages of compression, one or more stages of expansion and a heat addition between the end of compression and the beginning of expansion, part of the work done in expansion being employed to do the work of compression, and the remainder to provide the fluid reaction.

Describing the invention in a simple form as applied to aircraft, there is a compression apparatus, consisting of a compressor, which may be a blower type compressor, a cylinder compressor, or a combination of the two, by means of which air as the working fluid is compressed into a heating chamber where heat is added by the combustion of fuel. The air then expanding through apparatus designed to absorb sufficient of the work of expansion to drive the compressor, and which may consist of a turbine rotor, or cylinder expander or a combination of the two, and which is on the same shaft

[Price 1/-]

as, or connected with, the compressing mechanism. The air then passes through a suitably designed tunnel to the atmosphere, either having velocity as a result of its passage through expansion apparatus, of being capable of further expansion through suitably designed nozzles at the rear, or both.

In another form, a portion of the air only may expand through the expansion apparatus which drives the compression apparatus, and the remainder expands to the atmosphere providing fluid reaction.

In more particularly describing the invention in an aircraft adaption, I propose to use a centrifugal rotary vane blower or turbo-compressor as a compressor. The air intake is a tunnel situated in the nose of the aircraft and leading in an axial direction to the inlet orifice of blower. The gas is passed circumferentially through suitably designed passages or diffusers into the heating chamber, which is of suitable material, and probably lagged externally to conserve heat. Into this chamber are directed burners for oil fuel and any further necessary details of construction such as pilot burners, cleaning devices etc. At the rear of the heating chamber the gas passes through suitable nozzles to impinge on the buckets or blades of a De Laval or Curtis type turbine wheel, the latter being mounted on the same shaft as the compressor. The gas passes into a tunnel after leaving the turbine and is led to the rear, where the final stage of expansion to the atmosphere takes place through suitably designed nozzles.

The invention is not limited to the mechanism detailed above. For instance, instead of the air passing through apparatus for driving compressor after heating, it may pass through and give up some of its heat to the water in a steam boiler, the steam so generated being utilised to drive the compression mechanism by means of a steam turbine or other steam engine. This would then be a substitute for the gas turbine above specified.

Controlling means may include fuel control, gas flow control, or mechanical control of the speed of the blower and/or

---

Churchill Archives Centre, Churchill College, Cambridge.

Above and overleaf pages: Whittle's first patent.

its mover. The final emission of gas may perhaps be directionally controlled for manœuvring purposes. One or a plurality of the complete power units may be provided in a single vehicle or aircraft and they may to some extent be interdependent, e.g. a single turbine may operate subsidiary blowers etc.

It may be necessary to provide auxiliary apparatus for starting, fuel injections, lubrication or like purposes.

It will be clear that the invention gives scope for wide modification without departing from its principle as herein outlined.

Dated this 14th day of January, 1930.
F. WHITTLE.

COMPLETE SPECIFICATION.

Improvements relating to the Propulsion of Aircraft and other Vehicles.

I, FRANK WHITTLE, late of "Glenhaven", Regent Street, Coventry, and now of "Hill Crest" Dorrington, Lincoln, British Subject, do hereby declare the nature of this invention and in what manner the same is to be performed, to be particularly described and ascertained in and by the following statement:—

This invention relates to apparatus for propulsion of the type in which air is taken in, compressed, heated, and expelled with high velocity on re-expansion in order to provide a propulsive thrust.

The main object of this invention is to provide improved apparatus of the above mentioned type, and in particular improved means for driving the compressor.

According to the invention I provide means for propulsion of the above mentioned type characterised by the feature that the compressor is driven by a turbine, and that the pressure drop on expansion takes place in two stages, the first pressure drop taking place through the nozzles of the turbine, and the second pressure drop taking place through the propelling nozzles.

Describing the invention in a simple form as applied to aircraft, there is a compressor, preferably of the turbo-centrifugal type, by means of which air as the working fluid is compressed into a heating chamber where heat is added by the combustion of fuel. The air is then expanded through apparatus designed to absorb sufficient of the work of expansion to drive the compressor, and which consists of a turbine rotor, and which is on the same shaft as or connected with the compressing mechanism. The air then passes through a suitably designed tunnel or nozzles to the atmosphere, either having velocity as a result of its expansion through the expansion apparatus, or being capable of further expansion through suitably designed nozzles at the rear, or both.

The invention will now be described with aid of the accompanying drawing and diagram in which:—

Fig. 1 is a diagram showing the cycle of energy or thermal cycle on which the invention relies fundamentally.

Fig. 2 is a part-section showing diagrammatically a preferred form of the invention, applicable to the propulsion of aircraft.

The thermal cycle employed which is shown in Fig. 1 is a pressure-volume diagram in which:

AG represents the atmospheric line.
DC represents compression.
CE represents heating at constant pressure.
EF represents that portion of expansion which is utilised to do the work of compression.
FG represents the expansion to the atmosphere providing thrust by fluid reaction.

The device consists of a compressor having casing "1" intake passages 2, a rotor "3", with bucket rings "4" working in conjunction with stator bucket or nozzle rings "5" inside the casing "1" and centrifugal radial blading "7" and diffusers "8" through which the output is delivered under pressure through header or collector ring "9" into combustion or heating chambers "10" in which fuel is burnt. This may be heavy oil or other fuel burning at jets "11". The chambers "10" are preferably lagged or otherwise heat insulated to conserve heat energy, and perhaps lined with refractory material. The heated gases pass into a collector or header "12" from chambers "10" which are of any suitable number and disposition. From header "12" the gases expand through a turbine "13" with buckets "14" and stator "15", the turbine rotor "13" being fast on the spindle "16", which is also the driving spindle of the compressor rotor "3",

"7". From the turbine the gases further expand through nozzles "17" to the atmosphere in an axial direction.

Any suitable type of turbine may be used, but in order that the relatively high temperature proposed to be employed may be withstood, the buckets may be of some suitable refractory material.

The turbine drives the compressor direct as shown, but direct drive is not essential, any gearing or the like may of course be employed.

The air entering at "2" is first of all compressed by the bucket system "4" "5", and by blades "7". In the chambers "10" the air is heated at constant pressure and expands through the turbine "13" losing energy by driving the turbine and compressor. Its remaining pressure and velocity energy is then converted into velocity out of the nozzles "17", whereby reaction in the nature of axial thrust is set up according to the usual laws.

It can be demonstrated that the efficiency of this device conceived as a propulsive engine, will not be reduced by reduction of the density of the atmosphere, and owing to the low temperature of the upper atmosphere may actually be enhanced.

Controlling means may include fuel control, gas flow control, or mechanical control of the speed of the blower and/or its mover. The final emission of gas may perhaps be directionally controlled for manœuvering purposes.

It may be necessary to provide auxiliary apparatus for starting, fuel injections, lubrication or like purposes.

Having now particularly described and ascertained the nature of my said invention and in what manner the same is to be performed, I declare that what I claim is:—

1. Means for propulsion of the type described, characterised by the feature that the compressor is driven by a turbine, and that the pressure drop on expansion takes place in two stages, the first pressure drop taking place through the nozzles of the turbine, and the second pressure drop taking place through the propelling nozzles.

2. Means for propulsion according to Claim 1, in which a multi-stage turbine is employed.

3. A propulsion device in which a centrifugal turbo-compressor supplies compressed air to a heating chamber whence the air passes to drive a turbine which mechanically drives the compressor, and whence in turn the air and products of combustion escape to the atmosphere through passages which cause them to produce propulsive thrust.

4. A device according to claims 1 and 3, constructed and operating substantially as described with reference to Fig. 2 of the accompanying drawings.

Dated this 14th day of October, 1930.

F. WHITTLE.

Redhill: Printed for His Majesty's Stationery Office, by Love & Malcomson, Ltd.—1931.

347,206 COMPLETE SPECIFICATION 1 SHEET

[This Drawing is a reproduction of the Original on a reduced scale.]

Fig. 1.

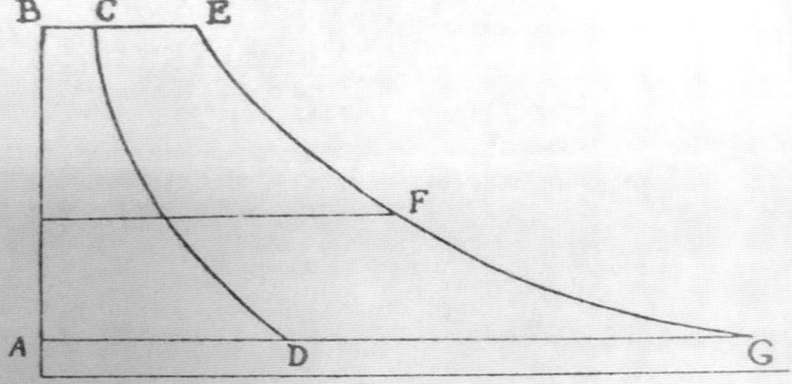

Fig. 2.

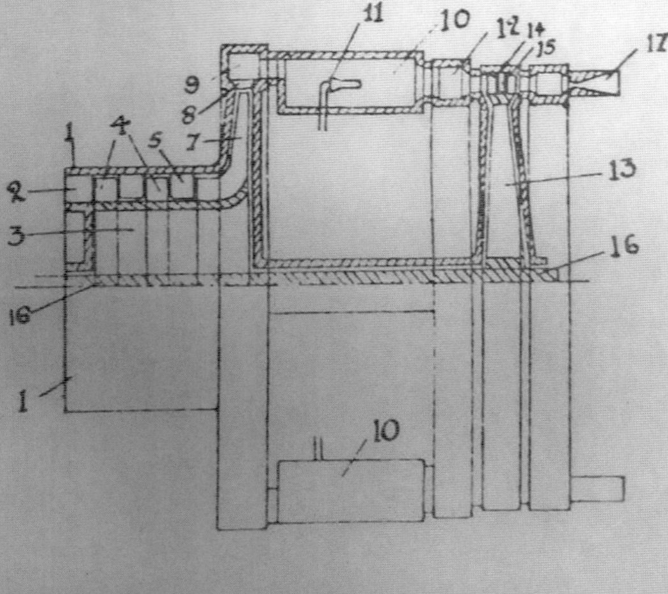

make it clear that they were now very interested in the new engine. They also said that they had told Rovers that they could "give them no assurances that there would not be a Rolls-Royce-Whittle unit making its appearance presently".[40]

In fact, during this visit Whittle was shown work going on by Rolls-Royce on a version of his engine with two rotors, in what looked like what is called today a 'ducted fan'. This was really a preview of how most current jet engines are now designed, although somewhat ironically current Rolls-Royce engines use three rotors, while their competitors have maintained their own versions of a two-rotor design. Seeing this advanced level of development at one of the largest and most capable manufacturing firms just added one more concern to the many other issues that were facing Whittle at the time.

At the end of June 1941, Hives and Stanley Hooker, a Rolls-Royce engineer, visited the Ladywood Works of Power Jets, and were impressed with the work being done in what were very primitive premises compared to their own factories. Whittle noted that 'Dr. Hooker expressed amazement at the absolute steadiness of the instruments' while observing Whittle's W1X engine on test.

After the exhilaration and excitement of the first successful flight test, Whittle found himself becoming almost overwhelmed by some of the problems emanating from the Air Ministry decision to provide engine component and assembly contracts to both BTH and Rover rather than directly to Power Jets. This was not only terribly disappointing to Whittle and the other directors of Power Jets, but also placed the full burden of design on Whittle while watching the other firms profit from his brilliant invention. In many ways the Power Jets directors felt quite helpless to control what had been their initiative in bringing jet propulsion to a commercial reality.

This naturally led to much dissatisfaction, and some internal squabbling within Power Jets by senior managers and directors.

In particular, the actions of Whyte, as managing director, was still causing Whittle considerable stress, and led to many disagreements. Some of these were perhaps minor in nature, but in the circumstances led to serious conflict, particularly between Whittle and Whyte.

Although the visit by Air Ministry officials at the beginning of the year had seemed to go well, by mid-1941 Power Jets was in upheaval. Whittle was still effectively in control, as he held the majority of the class 'A' shares in the company, with Col Tinling and Dudley-Williams as minor shareholders. He finally decided that Whyte would have to go, and wrote to Tinling and Dudley-Williams on 2 July 1941, explaining his decision to remove him.[41] In his letter, Whittle said that his decision to dismiss Whyte was based on two main grounds, namely;

1) That though Mr Whyte is a man of very considerable ability and energy, this is not of the type that fits him for his present position.
2) For various reasons (most of which are well known to you) he is unpopular with the senior members of the Company, to such a degree that the situation caused is seriously clogging development.

It has happened far too often that necessary steps have been taken only after considerable goading by myself and others – steps which could, and ought to, have been foreseen by one in his position.

I therefore think that you should initiate the necessary steps to bring his appointment to an end. In any case you should now make effective his formal resignation as Chairman, which is in your possession.

On the same day, Whittle wrote a lengthy letter directly to Whyte, explaining his reasons for withdrawing his support.[42] In his two-page letter, Whittle vented his frustrations, both major and minor, with Whyte at some length. It is worth quoting this letter in its entirety to fully understand Whittle's state of mind at the time, and his concern with any activities that seemed to be bordering on illegal, or at least unethical, behaviour.

Dear Whyte,

It is with great regret that I have to tell you I can no longer support your position as Managing Director of Power Jets.

The main reason for this step is that I am certain that you do not, and never will, command the loyalty of the senior members of the firm. A secondary reason is that though you have made many useful contributions to the development, your handling of many important matters to date has not, in my opinion, been as satisfactory as one has the right to expect from one in receipt of so large a salary.

I freely acknowledge that you are a man of very considerable ability and energy, and that you are an enthusiastic worker in any cause which you believe to serve the National Interest, but unfortunately, your particular abilities do not seem to be of the right type for efficient management of the affairs of a rapidly growing engineering organisation such as Power Jets.

I also realise that you have often received the blame for situations for which the Ministry of Aircraft Production has been really responsible, and you have been unfortunate in having to have dealings with individuals whose motives and business morals leave a lot to be desired, but even so it has happened far too often that necessary steps have been taken only after considerable 'goading' by myself and others, steps which could, and ought to have been foreseen by one in your position.

I attribute many difficulties to your faulty judgement, which has caused you to be over-impetuous in some matters, and to have been insufficiently active in others. (Under the heading of faulty judgement I place the case of the arbitration position in relation to the Rover Co. when you informed us that the Rover Co.'s agreement to arbitration had been secured, and where it subsequently transpired that the letter on which you relied had very little legal value.)

The attitude of the senior members of the staff towards you is a very serious matter, and there is no doubt that the hostility which I have observed so often is an active barrier between yourself and the individuals concerned, and it has been a major cause of lack of liaison and understanding. Coupled with this unpopularity is a marked lack of respect due, I think, mainly to the loss of dignity arising out of a number of minor avoidable actions which have caused much comment among the employees. Instances of these are:-

(1) You were seen driving Mrs. Whyte and your step-daughter in the Company's V.8 at Easter (or so I am informed).
You gave a cocktail party which is popularly supposed to have been for the purpose of obtaining 'paying guests' for the Rectory.
You were summoned for an offence in connection with aliens who have been in your employ as domestic servants at the Rectory.

There are many other incidents which have caused derogatory comment.

With the exception of (3) those I have quoted are very trivial, but they are nevertheless very potent in their effect on your standing in the eyes of the employees, and it seems to me that you do not realise that it is necessary to be, in your position, not only especially scrupulous, but to appear so in the eyes of all concerned.

I think it only fair that you should know your action in taking 'paying guests' has proved to be unfortunate in that you have made yourself the subject of discussion as a 'landlord'.

I personally take a more serious view of the employment of aliens as domestic servants because, though there is no legal reason why you should not do so, it appears to me obvious that it is a most unwise thing to do for one in your position, especially when at the time you had a serving officer and civil servant in the house.

I want you to know that this step is a very painful one to me, and that it is only with great reluctance that I take it, convinced as I am that it is absolutely essential for the good of the development.

I bear you no personal malice whatever and I hope most sincerely that your real abilities will find a more suitable employment in the very near future. I say further that I do not wish to see you break all your ties with a development in which you have undoubtedly played a prominent part, and (though I have no say in the matter in any case) I shall not resent your remaining on the Board of the Company.

Yours sincerely,

F. W.

Whittle's concerns with boarders was evidently related to the fact that the company had rented an old rectory near to the Power Jets facilities in Lutterworth for Whyte's use as managing director of the company. Whyte had been supplementing his salary from the company by taking in boarders to fill some of the spare rooms, and had also evidently hired some non-British 'aliens' as domestic servants.

Unsurprisingly, as a result of this devastating letter, Whyte duly resigned as chairman and managing director on 12 July 1941. Whittle, as the controlling shareholder of the company, then appointed Col Tinling as chairman and himself and Dudley-Williams as joint managing directors. All of these issues were clearly starting to affect Whittle's health, and his reputation for being a 'stickler' was also beginning to have an effect on him. For example, at the end of a letter to Major Bulman, in the Ministry of Aircraft Production, Whittle complains that, 'Similarly, before I have ever met certain individuals someone has managed to convey the impression that I am difficult to get on with, etc, etc. These things are undoubtedly impeding the development and something must be done to stop it.'

Meanwhile, with the introduction of the Lubbock-style atomising combustion chamber, the engine performance had improved dramatically, and testing focused on improving reliability and increasing the engine thrust. By mid-1941 the staff of Power Jets had grown to nearly 150, including designers as well as engineers and technicians involved in engine testing. While testing continued with the original WU engine as well as the W1X production prototype, the design team was fully engaged in the design of the next generation engine, the W2, which would eventually form the basis for the first successful production engine, the W2B. This engine had been designed by Whittle and his team to power the new twin-engined Gloster Meteor, which had been commissioned by the Air Ministry specifically to utilise Whittle's new jet engine.

To Whittle's great disappointment, however, orders from the Air Ministry for production versions of the W2B went directly to the Rover company, which had by now established a new jet engine production line, as well as component manufacturing facilities, at its Barnoldswick factory in Lancashire, close to the Yorkshire Dales. In late October 1941, the Ministry of Aircraft Production (MAP) agreed that Power Jets should be equipped to make experimental engines. Whittle was very disappointed, however, to learn that the MAP was expecting production engines to be manufactured by the existing major engine manufacturers, such as Rolls-Royce. This was really the end of the line for the dream that Whittle and the other company directors had of Power Jets becoming a major jet engine manufacturer.

At the end of October 1941, a small delegation from Rolls-Royce, including Stanley Hooker, visited Whittle at his Ladywood Works. The visitors asked Whittle for his opinion on their 'scheme', which used an axial-flow compressor rather than Whittle's somewhat cumbersome radial compressor. Whittle suggested that their design was 'very ambitious', but they may just 'get away with it'. He also discussed at some length the 'surging difficulties' that Power Jets had experienced, and suggested that a joint design effort with Rolls-Royce might be advantageous. The visitors seemed to like this suggestion and described in some detail their plans for the now ubiquitous 'straight-through' design, which seemed to be less susceptible to the surging problem. About a week after this visit Power Jets were asked to send their wooden mock-up of a W2B engine to Vickers-Armstrongs to facilitate the future installation of the actual engine in a Wellington Mark IV bomber for testing.

At this time there was also a great deal of back and forth discussion between Power Jets and the MAP about collaboration with other firms in order to fast-track quantity production of the new engine. In early November Whittle learned that Rover had received notice from the MAP that they were to deliver twelve W2B engines by the end of the year for installation and testing in four of the new Meteors. The fact that Rover, rather than Power Jets, had received this 'production' order, added to the stress that Whittle was increasingly feeling. Shortly after this, Whittle wrote to Hives, asking for manufacturing help from Rolls-Royce, and 'closer collaboration in the future'. Also, at the end of 1941, Hayne Constant at the Royal Aircraft Establishment (RAE) wrote a note to Whittle in which he said that 'there is no doubt that an axial-flow compressor is best for use in gas'.

At the end of 1941 the Ministry made the critical decision to send one of Whittle's latest designs of engines, the W1X, to the US. This engine was given to General Electric, who used it to work on a design for a very similar engine. Some six months later the engineers at GE ran their very first jet engine, which they called the 1-A. In late 1942 GE used two of their 1-A engines to power the specially built Bell XP-59A Airacomet, which marked the beginning of the US becoming a major manufacturer of jet-powered aircraft. This, of course, enabled General Electric, one of the largest manufacturing companies in the US, to become a major manufacturer of jet engines. This continues today, with GE being one of the dominant manufacturers of such engines in the world. They are direct competitors with Rolls-Royce in the UK, and Pratt & Whitney, also in the US.

By the end of 1941 all the stress that had been building on Whittle came to a head. By this time he had spent years dedicated to getting his ground-breaking engine concept from the drawing board to practical reality without having time to sustain a normal family or social life. In addition, he had naturally found all of the wrangling over the future of Power Jets, and its likely role in commercial development of the jet engine, to be completely exhausting. He was tired, both physically and mentally, from the years of single-minded dedication to bringing his dream to reality and from the seemingly endless skirmishes and battles with legions of Air Ministry officials and government advisors. This had been compounded by the endless internal wrangling within Power Jets related to Whyte's handling of the company's affairs and his subsequent resignation. Not surprisingly then, just some six months after the exhilaration of the first flight of the E.28/39, Whittle's brilliant mind became overloaded and he had the second of what would be a series of 'nervous breakdowns', as any form of mental distress was described in those days. As a result, on 11 December 1941, Whittle entered the military hospital set up at St Hughes College, Oxford, and did not return to work again until early in the New Year.

At the very end of the year, on 30 December, with Whittle in the hospital, Dudley-Williams, Tinling and Johnson visited the MAP to meet with the Minister, John Moore Brabazon (later Lord Brabazon of Tara). The Power Jets visitors complained to the Minister that they were finding relations with the Rover company were deteriorating. They suggested that Rover was acting independently and were starting to make some changes to Whittle's design without consultation. They clearly believed that Rover should just be manufacturing engines strictly to Power Jets' design without making any of their own modifications. They were naturally quite taken aback when the Minister told them that Rover were responsible for their 'own' production without reference to Power Jets. He went on to say that Power Jets were to be responsible for doing any research required by Rover, and other potential manufacturers, and should be available to act as 'consultants' to the much larger manufacturing companies. This was not, of course, what the Power Jets team was hoping to hear, and they returned to Lutterworth in a very discouraged mood. As they were leaving the Minister they suggested that they were very reluctant to act as 'consultants' to Rover as their advice was never taken.

In a further complication to Whittle's plans, Ernest Hives, at Rolls-Royce aero engines, was rapidly making plans to move into the jet engine business. Hives had a background much like Whittle, and had started his working life as a mechanic. He joined Rolls-Royce, then just a motorcar manufacturer, after repairing one of C.S. Rolls' early cars. From there he went on to become a test driver for Rolls, and then head of the experimental department that developed early Rolls-Royce aero engines. Ultimately he became chairman of Rolls-Royce Ltd and was ennobled as the first Baron Hives in 1950. Hives was also a very shrewd businessman and realised that although the Merlin piston engine had proved to be a brilliant design and powered many of Britain's combat aircraft during the war, it had reached its limits of development and the future was likely to be with the jet engine pioneered by Whittle.

Shortly after returning to work in January 1942, Whittle was invited by Hives to visit the Rolls-Royce factory in Derby. Whittle and Hives, with similar working-class backgrounds, got on very well. Hives had been the driving force behind the development and production of the Merlin. Air Chief Marshal Sir Wilfred Freeman said of him, 'That man Hives is the best man I have ever come across for many a year. God knows where the RAF would have been without him. He cares for nothing except the defeat of Germany, and he does all his work to that end, living a life of unending labour.'[43]

On 14 January 1942, just after Whittle returned to work from the hospital, a small group of senior Rolls-Royce engineers, including Stanley Hooker and George Elliott, the chief engineer, visited the Ladywood Works. They held discussions with the Power Jets team and indicated that Rolls-Royce were 'seriously considering constructing the Whittle type unit'. Less than a week later, after having discussions with the senior Rolls-Royce management, they again returned to Lutterworth. At the meeting with senior Power Jets partners Elliott said that he 'regretted not getting in touch with Whittle four years ago'. He also said that in his opinion, 'in 10 years' time the reciprocating engine would be a back number as far as aviation was concerned'. In retrospect, this meeting really marked the beginning of Rolls-Royce becoming one of the largest and most important companies designing and manufacturing jet engines to this day. As they were leaving, Elliott said that Rolls-Royce were very interested in building a unit 'on W2B lines', but with modifications that he would like to discuss with Whittle.

A week after this meeting, Whittle went with a small team from Power Jets to visit Rolls-Royce at their headquarters in Derby. They met a small team led by Hives, who got straight into the discussion by saying that the 'Whittle Unit' was now equal to or better that the Merlin 61. This was an astonishing admission, given that the Merlin at that time was the peak of Rolls-Royce achievements. Hives said that Rolls-Royce would take all advice they could from Whittle, but at the end of the day they would develop their own version of the W2B with or without his help. This was, of course, very difficult for Whittle to hear, as he had thought that this meeting could result in some form of direct collaboration between the two companies, one the established leader in aircraft propulsion, and the other a small, but promising newcomer to the table.

A week later, Hives and Rolls-Royce managing director Arthur Sidgreaves visited the Power Jets facilities in Lutterworth, and were no doubt taken aback by the very small facilities compared to those of their company. During their meeting with Whittle and other senior Power Jets managers, Hives said that after the war there would be 'an absolute glut' of Merlin engines, and Rolls-Royce intended to pursue the new jet propulsion concepts pioneered by Whittle.

Hives realised that after the end of the war there may be little interest in conventional piston-driven aeroplane engines, like the Merlin, however successful they may have been. He knew from discussions at a very high level in the Ministry of Aircraft Production that there may well be a shift towards the new type of jet propulsion engines pioneered by Whittle. As a key contractor to the Air Ministry, and subsequently the MAP run by Lord Beaverbrook, he was also well aware of the work being done by Rover and BTH in building experimental engines to Whittle's design.

The two men had a good discussion about the future prospects for jet engine manufacturing, and Hives suggested that Rolls-Royce would very likely be keen on some type of cooperation with Whittle and Power Jets.

Hives was clearly concerned that Whittle might be looking for a commercial tie-up with another firm, such as Rover, which would make it much more difficult for Rolls-Royce to pursue the commercialisation of jet propulsion to the fullest extent possible. Whittle, however, was likely quite naive about commercial matters, and didn't press Hives at that time for any kind of commercial link between the two firms, which could have been very beneficial for Power Jets shareholders. Whittle told Hives that Power Jets had 'kept clear of entanglements to date' because they were determined to remain their independence as a design and manufacturing company.[44] Hives seemed to be reassured that Power Jets wasn't planning a commercial tie up with Rovers, or any other firm, and didn't make any kind of formal offer of a more direct commercial linkage between Rolls-Royce and Power Jets.

The following day Whittle travelled to Derby, the headquarters of Rolls-Royce, for further talks with Hives. During the meeting Whittle suggested that there were still some unsubscribed shares available in Power Jets, in a first indication that these could be bought by Rolls-Royce in order to have a major influence on the future commercial development of jet propulsion. Hives did not, however, jump at the chance of taking up these shares, perhaps because he had been reassured in the previous day's meeting that Whittle was not pursuing a commercial tie-up with any other firms. Whittle noted that 'In general, I received the impression that their eagerness of the day before had cooled off somewhat.'[45] This was probably the moment when Power Jets lost any realistic chance of becoming a major commercial player in the exciting future of jet powered flight.

It may have been Hives' impression that he had opened the door to future collaboration, and perhaps even a commercial relationship, and that the next move was up to Whittle. This was probably the time when Whittle had the greatest opportunity to put Power Jets on a firm path to the future by negotiating a commercial agreement with Rolls-Royce. Unfortunately, however, Whittle thought that the next move should come from Hives, but in the end there was no follow-up. In retrospect, had Whittle pursued some form of commercial tie-up between Power Jets and Rolls-Royce it could have set the stage for a very profitable joint venture. The result may well have enabled Whittle and his colleagues at Power Jets to benefit financially in a very significant way from the joint development of his engine. However, Whittle was probably still too much the serving RAF officer to appreciate the full commercial potential that such an arrangement might provide for him and his colleagues at Power Jets. In any event, the MAP had other plans for Power Jets.

At this time Whittle was already looking beyond the successful W2B design, and was working with his team of Power Jets designers on an improved version designed for large-scale production, which he named the W2/500. This engine had essentially the same layout as the W2B but several design changes were made to improve its reliability and increase the thrust to 1,750lb.

One of the difficulties of increasing thrust without changing the engine size is the increased aerodynamic loading, which can be particularly difficult for the compressor. Compressor design is very challenging, since the objective is to produce as large an increase in pressure as possible from the low-pressure inlet conditions to the high-pressure outlet in as short a space as possible while maintaining a high flow rate. One of the challenges with Whittle's earlier designs had been compressor 'surging', which can occur under high load when compressor blades become momentarily stalled aerodynamically, thereby greatly reducing airflow through the engine. Aerodynamic stall results from the airflow separating from the blade surface when the angle of attack is too high. This separation tends to produce regions of air recirculation, rather than the desirable 'attached' flow, resulting in reduced overall airflow throughout the compressor. With the reduced airflow the compressor blades then recover from their stalled condition and the airflow once more builds up to the point where the blades stall again. Rapid repetition of these events causes the surging phenomena with highly varying flow rates and pressures throughout the engine, and can lead to catastrophic failure of engine components. This dangerous phenomena can often be reduced or eliminated altogether by changing blade angles and/or reducing the blade aerodynamic loading in the compressor. Whittle had learned much about this phenomena, however, in his many attempts to increase engine output. As a result, he found that by carefully specifying compressor blade angles he could eliminate the dangerous compressor stall condition across the complete performance envelope.

Whittle wrote to Air Vice-Marshal Francis Linnell, Controller of R&D in the MAP, on 20 January 1942, giving an upbeat summary of progress to date on the W2B engine. He indicated that the engine gave very good performance up to 16,500 rpm, but was limited by 'surging' at 17,000 rpm. At full speed it provided a thrust of 1,415lb, and Whittle suggested that 'the most serious aerodynamic and thermodynamic troubles' had now been overcome. He also noted that this gave about the same performance as the latest Rolls-Royce Merlin model 61 engine, although the W2B engine weighed 750lb compared to the Merlin's 2,500lb. The very significant improvement in power-to-weight ratio was obviously an important advantage for the new engine design.

This period really marked the time at which all of Whittle's hard work, despite the many frustrations he had encountered, finally proved that he had been vindicated in his unshakable faith in the ultimate superiority of his brilliant new engine design when compared to the best conventional piston engine then in production. A week later, Whittle again wrote to Linnell with some suggestions for volume manufacturing of his new engine, which for the first time he suggested should be named the Welland. He said this was the name of the legendary Smith of Kent described in Anglo-Saxon folklore. Somewhat ironically, Rolls-Royce would later adopt the name Welland for its first production engine, previously known as the Power Jets W2B. This appears to be the first instance of their policy, still in use today, of naming their engines after British rivers. The current family of large jet engines are known as Trent, named after the river that runs through the Midlands.

Following the disappointing meetings with Rolls-Royce, which proved to be rather unproductive in terms of future commercialisation of his engine, Whittle returned his focus to the latest Power Jets engine design. He had designed the W2/500 with a larger turbine diameter and fewer blades with a greater chord, or blade width. This proved to be very beneficial, and the new design resulted in a major improvement in performance. The new engine design also benefitted from the use of much stronger and more durable turbine blades. These were made from a new nickel alloy known as Nimonic 80, which had been developed by the International Nickel Company (INCO) at their Wiggin works in Hereford. This factory had originally been the site of Henry Wiggin and Co., a pioneering developer of high-temperature alloys. These high-nickel alloys proved to be very robust in such a sustained high-temperature environment, and similar materials are still used today to provide the high reliability required of all jet engines. Only some six months after the redesign had begun the new engine was run on a test stand,

and achieved its full design thrust of 1,750lb, nearly double that of the original WU engine design.

Meanwhile, the other firms who had been working with Whittle were clearly planning on becoming major players in this exciting new industry after the war. In April 1942 Whittle was shocked and very upset to learn that without consulting him Rover had been working on a new version of the W2B engine with a 'straight-through' combustion system, which they called the W2B/26. This featured combustion chambers in which the air and ultimately combustion products moved directly from inlet to outlet in a straight line without the reverse-flow design used in all Whittle's engines to date. This resulted in a longer engine, but greatly simplified the combustion chamber design and reduced flow losses associated with the flow reversals in the Power Jets design. Whittle himself had already envisaged such an arrangement for future development, but had not yet proceeded with a detailed design due to the pressing need to improve performance of his original engine.

Rover had been working on this engine at their Clitheroe design office, which was near to the former cotton mill in Barnoldswick, Lancashire, that Rover had taken over in 1941 in order to manufacture jet engines. This design used the same compressor and turbine design as in the W2B/23, but an elongated shaft connecting the two had enabled the use of 'straight-through' combustion chambers. In Whittle's 'reverse-flow' design air from the compressor entered the combustion chambers near the front of the engine and moved towards the back of the chamber, where the flow then reversed direction before being mixed with fuel and ignited. The combustion products were then redirected back towards the rear of the engine through a U-bend before entering the turbine section (see Plate 11). Although Whittle realised that this resulted in substantial pressure losses, the design resulted in a very compact engine design and eliminated the need for a central bearing to support the shaft joining the compressor to the turbine. Unbeknownst to Whittle, however, Rover's senior design engineer, Adrian Lombard, had reworked this design by increasing the distance between compressor and turbine, enabling the use of 'straight-through' combustion chambers in which air and combustion products always moved from the front to the rear of the engine. The engine ended up being longer overall, however, and necessitated the use of a central shaft support bearing.

This design ultimately ended up being put into production by Rolls-Royce as the RB/26 Derwent engine (see Plate 15) and superseded the Welland, with most Meteors being powered by the engine.

Whittle had always envisaged that the 'straight-through' configuration may be a future alternative version of his engine, but was infuriated that Rover had gone ahead with a complete redesign without his knowledge. When he found out about this it naturally put a great strain on his relationship with Rover, and with senior MAP personnel, who he realised must have authorised this change without reference to Power Jets.

This was just another example of the worsening relations between Whittle and the Rover company, which officials at the Air Ministry were getting increasingly frustrated about. In a memo to the Ministry, Whittle said that he would reluctantly continue working with the company if necessary, but that 'under normal circumstances I would have no relations whatever with individuals of the calibre of the brothers Wilks'. Despite saying this, however, Whittle did have a good opinion of some of the key engineers working at Rover. In particular, he was impressed with Adrian Lombard, who went on to have a very successful career with Rolls-Royce. At the time, however, the 'go-it-alone' approach of Rovers on this new design without even consulting Whittle added to the great mental strain he was already feeling.

Chapter 7

Visit to the USA

The increasing frequency of actions being taken by others to redesign and 'improve' his basic concept without consulting him was beginning to take a toll on Whittle. It was also distracting him from giving 100 per cent of his attention to development work. On 12 April 1942, Whittle wrote a long letter to Air Marshal Linnell in which he complained about being left out of major decisions on alternative new engine concepts, such as the 'straight-through' design. He ended his letter by telling Linnell, 'In light of the foregoing remarks, and the history of events I feel entitled to request either that matters of policy affecting the progress of the venture should be discussed with me before they are laid down, or I should be informed definitely of what I already have grounds for suspecting, namely, that my judgement and experience in such matters is believed to be inept. In the latter event it would appear that but little useful purpose could be achieved by my remaining in my present position.'[46]

Whittle's letter clearly had the effect intended, and a week later Linnell wrote back to Whittle, as follows:

Dear Whittle,

You will not expect me to answer your letter of April 12th at length. I prefer to await an opportunity for discussion with yourself and one of your associates which I intend to arrange very shortly.

This I can say, however, in regard to the purpose of your letter, which was to request that you should have a hearing before any changes in policy are made. I can re-assure you that no changes of policy are in contemplation, and I hope that any arrangement which I shall make will ensure that you are kept fully in the picture in future when any changes of design are under discussion. That there will have to be modifications of the design from time to time must be accepted and it may be that for good reasons the design which seems to you the best may not be acceptable on grounds of production, maintenance, etc. Nevertheless, before any decisions on a matter of this kind are to be made, it will be my purpose to ensure that your views are taken fully into account.

Yours sincerely,
F.J. Linnell[47]

Work on a somewhat revised design of Whittle's engine had also been started at the De Havilland company, better known for their work in designing and building aircraft. This had been designed primarily by Frank Halford, a very skilled engineer who had taken great interest in Whittle's activities. He no doubt knew about Whittle's engine design from his company's attendance at the frequent industry collaboration meetings hosted by the Ministry of Aircraft Production. As a result, Halford produced his own design with some help from Power Jets employees, but with very little reference to Whittle. His engine was different from Whittle's design in one important way, in that it incorporated a 'straight-through' combustion system utilising sixteen individual combustion chambers. It was, of course, longer than Whittle's engine, but it had the benefit of eliminating the complications of the reverse-flow characteristics of Whittle's engine. This simpler 'straight-through' combustion chamber design is now incorporated in all current jet engine designs. As Halford's engine became closer to a production reality, he had some correspondence with Whittle in which he alluded to the rather cool relationship between De Havilland and Power Jets. On 14 May 1942, he wrote to Whittle in an attempt to improve their collaboration by telling him that he had begun his engine design at the invitation of the Ministry of Aircraft Production.[48] He said, 'To be quite frank I have always regretted that there has not been a better atmosphere between us. I consistently obtained the impression, admittedly second-hand, that you rather resented the work we were doing, whereas I was only carrying out the request made by Sir Henry Tizard, who was so insistent in my taking an interest in the work you had been doing.'

He ended his letter by saying, 'To finalise my views, for some regrettable reason or other, we started off in a bad atmosphere but this has improved very considerably with time, and I hope sincerely that this improvement will continue.'

Whittle clearly appreciated the letter from Halford, and ended a lengthy reply by saying, 'I am very glad to see that you feel that relations between us have improved very considerably with time, and I share your hope that this improvement will continue.'[49]

This was just another example of the great strain that Whittle was under at the time as he could see that others were beginning to take control of his invention, in many cases with little reference to his original work.

Air Marshal Linnell had also written a more formal letter to Power Jets, in which he confirmed his remarks to Whittle that he and his colleagues should be consulted whenever major design changes were being contemplated. He said, 'I wish to make it clear in the first place that my policy remains what it was, namely the maintenance of full cooperation between all the firms concerned, and in particular between yourselves and Messrs. Rover. It is my expressed intention that Wing Commander Whittle should be kept informed of any intended changes of design. That such collaboration has been jeopardized by the way in which this matter has been handled I fully agree, and I am taking steps to ensure that a failure in this respect, which is fatal to a policy of collaboration, shall not recur.'[50]

Although these reassurances may have helped to assuage Whittle's worst fears, it did not really result in putting the 'genie back in the bottle' in order to give Whittle full control of future design modifications.

The Air Ministry recognised that large established companies such as Rover and Rolls-Royce would be best equipped to take on large-scale manufacturing of production versions of Whittle's now proven jet engine. They recognised, however that Whittle and Power Jets still had a valuable role to play in the design and experimental development of new versions of the nascent jet engine. As a result, in October 1941 they had provided the funds for a new factory for Power Jets at Whetstone just south of Leicester, and some 10 miles north of Lutterworth, for the production and testing of experimental engines. This new facility was completed within a year and was a huge improvement over the cramped facilities at Lutterworth. Whittle had no significant role in the planning and development of the new factory, in part due to his ongoing health issues and in part due to his extensive travel commitments. When he first visited the site, he was astonished by its size and the large complement of machine tools and other facilities that had been provided specifically for the manufacture and testing of jet engines.

As the Air Ministry became increasingly convinced that the jet engine would be the new standard for aircraft propulsion, they believed that they should share this information with their key ally, the USA, in order to help speed the end of the war. The US had been supporting the British government both financially and with materials for the war effort, and there was likely some thought within the British government that they should help to repay this by bringing the US into the jet age. They therefore decided to send a complete jet engine to the US, together with several Power Jets employees to help explain its design to interested US firms. As General Electric were already heavily involved in designing and manufacturing turbo-superchargers for piston aircraft engines, it was thought that they would be the most likely to take up an interest in jet propulsion. As a result, on 1 October 1941, the W1X experimental engine that had been such a wonderful workhouse for Power Jets was shipped to GE together with a complete set of drawings and three Power Jets employees. This would turn out to be the genesis of GE becoming one of the largest and most successful manufacturers of jet engines to this day.

In early 1942, the Air Ministry had suggested that Whittle should fly to the US in order to visit GE and to meet with others in the US who may be interested in developing the jet engine. They may also have believed that such a trip would relieve Whittle of some of the incredible stress he had been under to bring his invention to fruition, and a trip to the US might provide him with a degree of rest and relaxation that he sorely needed. With Rover now well advanced with production of the W2B at their Barnoldswick factory, and development work well under way by Power Jets at Whetstone on the W2/500, Whittle was happy to take a break and travel to the US.

He arrived on 4 June 1942, and the next day began his visit to the Lynn Works of GE in Lynn, Massachusetts. This was a huge factory that had been heavily involved in building turbo-superchargers (now commonly called 'turbochargers') for conventional piston-driven aircraft engines. He found the factory to be bustling and very modern, and was especially impressed with the wide range of up-to-date machine tools. He also found all of the GE senior managers and engineers that he met to be extremely friendly and welcoming. They bombarded him with a wide range of questions about his radical new engine and were particularly keen to understand what improvements to the original design he may be able to recommend. Following this very successful visit to GE he was taken to other factories in Schenectady and Buffalo, New York, and to the Air Force research laboratory in Dayton, Ohio. He found the work at Schenectady to be particularly interesting, since they were building a turboprop engine in which a gas turbine engine is used to drive a conventional propeller, rather than to produce a high-speed jet of exhaust gases. This was a concept that Whittle had already envisaged, but had not proceeded with in England because of his limited time and resources. After his visit Whittle said that he was very impressed with GE, and added that they considered the jet engine 'proved'.

Finally, Whittle's 'official' duties concluded with a cross-continent trip to visit senior managers and engineers at the Northrop Aircraft Inc. factory in Los Angeles. Northrop had been founded just before the war, and so were not nearly as experienced as the other companies that Whittle had visited in the US. Nevertheless, they had embarked on an ambitious programme to develop their own version of a turbo-propeller engine and were keen to get Whittle's opinion of their efforts to date. This was difficult for Whittle because he quickly realised that they were out of their depth, and did not really have the resources or skills to design and build a successful engine. Although he felt awkward doing so, he nevertheless told the company founder, Jack Northrop, that the design they were working on was far too complicated, and unlikely to be successful without a major redesign. Afterwards he was relieved to learn that his remarks likely had not caused offence as Northrop had dropped their turboprop engine project altogether.[51] By this time Whittle was feeling the effects of the hectic travel schedule, and had sometimes found the questioning so intense that it was quite exhausting. He was beginning to feel a little overwhelmed and worried that he may be falling back into the type of depression that he had experienced so recently back in England. This was clearly noticed by his hosts, however, and so a genuine holiday was planned for the remainder of his stay in Los Angeles.

Whittle had been staying at the Miramar Hotel in Santa Monica, and the local British consulate suggested that he stay on for a few days and just enjoy himself. However, 'just enjoying himself' had not been one of Whittle's habits for a very long time, and after a few days on his own he felt that he really should get back to work. When he asked the consulate to arrange for his return home, however, he found that they had other ideas for him. The British Air Commission representative in the consulate, Group Captain James Adams, had good connections with the ex-patriot British community in Los Angeles. Adams immediately had Whittle check out of the Miramar Hotel, and took him just a few miles away and checked him into the Beverly Hills Hotel, even today the best-known hotel in the US for attracting celebrities. After Whittle had settled in, Adams picked him up and took him to the nearby home of Edward ('Eddie') Hillman Jr, where Adams was a house guest. Eddie's third wife was the well-known British dancer and actress June Howard-Tripp, formerly Lady Inverclyde. Her previous husband, John Allan Burns, was the 4th Baron Inverclyde and the great-grandson of Sir George Burns, founder of the Cunard Line. Cunard became famous for transporting several generations of well-heeled passengers back and forth across the Atlantic. June was Burns' second wife, but he had no children by either spouse and the title was extinguished when Inverclyde died in 1957. June had previously appeared on both the stage in London and in films, including Alfred Hitchcock's *The Lodger*. Eddie was the heir to the Hillman's Chicago Department Store, and was said to have inherited $3 million in 1937, equivalent to approximately $50 million today. He and June were very well connected with the Hollywood 'set', and seemed to spend most of their time arranging parties and entertaining a wide variety of show business guests. After the US entered the war Eddie became a captain in the US Army Air Force as an intelligence officer.

For the next ten days Whittle became a frequent guest at the Hillmans' home on North Maple Drive, just a few blocks from the Beverly Hills Hotel. He unexpectedly found himself becoming much more relaxed and thoroughly enjoyed meeting a wide range of the couple's guests, which included many members of the Hollywood entertainment industry. This was perhaps the first time that Whittle had experienced a way of life that was completely alien to his own. He found, however, that he adapted quickly and very much enjoyed the sunshine and seemingly endless parties around the swimming pool. These sometimes lasted well into the early hours, with guests moving back and forth between the dining room and the pool, often until 3am! He later said, 'My diary of the remainder of my stay in California is very sketchy, and my memories of it are somewhat disjointed. I found the treatment, with the sun, rest etc., very congenial, so much so, that after 10 days I felt the urge to return to work.'[46] After his well-deserved holiday in the glitz of Hollywood, Whittle flew to Washington DC for a brief visit before travelling back to Britain. Here he met various government agencies and provided them with his generally positive impressions of the work on US jet engine development. He then flew back home, arriving in London on 14 August 1942. He had been in the US for nearly two and a half months by this time, and although he had thoroughly enjoyed his time there, he was ready to get back to work.

Upon his return to the UK Whittle told Wing Commander Watt that the attitude to jet development in the US was 'much more positive than in the UK'. He said that the whole venture was 'imperilled by dispersal of effort instead of concentration', in a sign of frustration that other companies in the UK were beginning to take a lead in jet engine production. He suggested that 'either the USA would become the only source of engines, or that an earthquake has to happen in the MAP'. Ironically, just six weeks after Whittle returned to the UK, a Bell Airacomet fighter plane, with two GE jet engines, made the first jet-propelled flight in the US. The GE 1-A engine had a full-power thrust of 1,250lb, identical to that of Whittle's W1 engine. A slightly modified version of this engine was then developed by GE to produce a thrust of 1,400lb, and became known as the type I-14.

Hap Arnold, commanding general of the US Army Air Force, had ordered the development of the Airacomet after seeing the Gloster E.28/39 fly in England in 1941. It first flew from the Muroc Army Airfield in California (now Edwards Air Force Base) on 2 October 1942, with Robert Stanley, the chief test pilot at Bell Aircraft at the controls. The plane had actually 'hopped' off the runway a few days earlier, but the first official flight was delayed for two days so that a number of observers and high-ranking air force officers could be present. This was the very first jet-engined flight in the US, which resulted in the dawn of the new jet age there, and heralded the beginning of GE's major role in jet engine design and manufacturing in the US and ultimately resulted in the company becoming one of the world's leading producers of jet engines. Although the Airacomet was the first US jet to fly, it was found to be under-powered compared to conventional fighters of the day. Production versions were ultimately withdrawn from service until newer and more powerful jet engines became available.

Chapter 8

Jet Engine Production Begins

Shortly after his arrival back from the US, Whittle met Roxbee Cox and Wing Commander Watt at the MAP. He provided them with his impressions of the jet engine work now going on in the US and told them he believed they were going ahead at great speed and would soon have a jet engine in operation. He told them he had been impressed by the enthusiasm of the engineers at GE, who seemed to already feel that jet propulsion was proven and should be available for the next generation of aircraft. He said that he was somewhat concerned that they may be going ahead too quickly with large-scale production plans without sufficient development and testing. The I-16 engine being built by GE was based closely on Whittle's W2/500 design and he believed that GE had plans to start large-scale production very soon. He then went on to discuss his own position following an inference from Roxbee Cox that he was seen as a Power Jets employee, rather than as a serving RAF officer. Whittle said that he 'objected most strongly' to this suggestion, and indicated that he looked upon Power Jets as a government organisation rather than as a commercial company. He also told Roxbee Cox that he believed 'the whole gas turbine project had been funded with tax-payers money, and ought to be the tax-payers property'.[47]

Shortly after his meeting at the MAP, Whittle again wrote to Roxbee Cox to give him the results of the first acceptance test of the new Power Jets W2/500 engine. He indicated that the engine had run for eight hours and achieved its full design thrust of 17,500lb. He ended his report by indicating with some pride that the engine had been run at its full design speed and thrust just six months after the design had begun. Roxbee Cox was clearly impressed and wrote a brief congratulatory note the following day in which he said, 'I am informing all concerned of the remarkable performance you have achieved and of the excellent agreement with the design predictions. I have no technical comments to make at the moment, and have nothing more to say but to congratulate you once again on a very impressive achievement.'[48] Whittle, who had great respect for Roxbee Cox, would have been very pleased with these comments. Two weeks later Roxbee Cox wrote again to Power Jets, authorising them to build three copies of the W2/500 engine, one of which would be used for flight trials in the E.28/39.

The very successful test results for the W2/500 led the MAP to consider production of this engine on a scale much larger than could be envisaged at the modest facilities of Power Jets. The department began to encourage the established aircraft engine manufacturers to take an interest in large-scale production of Whittle's engine, and as a result Ernest Hives of Rolls-Royce and a colleague visited Power Jets in early October 1942. Hives was shown the most recent test results and asked about the performance of this engine in comparison to Halford's H1 with the 'straight-through' combustion system. Whittle indicated that he believed the H1 was still in early development and didn't have the combustion stability and weight-to-thrust ratio of the compact 'reverse-flow' design embodied in his W2/500 engine.

The Power Jets memo recording the meeting ended with the suggestion that, 'It was said that there had been a suggestion between Rolls-Royce and Rover that they should swap jobs on the "Gyrone" and Meteor tank engines; this was suggested as evidence that Rover would like to get out of the "Gyrone" field. The attitude seemed to be that Rolls-Royce are now in this field and are going to stay in; but they wish to be on work which enthuses them and for that reason they must be satisfied that what they build is the right job.'[49]

As it would turn out, this is exactly what would later happen, much to the benefit of Rolls-Royce and the detriment of Rover. Shortly after Hives' visit, Power Jets received a letter from the MAP indicating that they would provide the funds for construction of a further twelve examples of the W2/500, confirming their wish to see this become a fully-fledged production design as quickly as possible.

In early December 1942, Whittle was summoned to a meeting with Air Chief Marshal Sir Wilfrid Freeman, the Air Member for Development and Production in the Ministry of Aircraft Production. This Ministry had been established in 1940 by the Canadian-born press baron Lord Beaverbrook, a great friend of Churchill's, to expand and expedite the badly needed fleet of fighters and bombers for the war in the air. Earlier in his career Freeman had been instrumental in ordering the Hawker Hurricane and Supermarine Spitfire, both of which proved so successful in defending the country in the Battle of Britain. Freeman had held increasingly important roles in the rapidly growing RAF and now had ultimate responsibility for all matters concerned with aircraft and aero engine development. The crux of the meeting was that Freeman wanted to know what Whittle thought of the prospect of bringing Rolls-Royce on board to seriously expedite the production of jet engines, which he now knew to be the future of aircraft propulsion. He suggested to Whittle that Rover had not really made much progress with making the engine suitable for mass production, and he was contemplating bringing the resources of both Rover and Power Jets together under the ultimate control of Rolls-Royce. Whittle thought that Freeman was looking to him to agree with this proposal, and then work with the newly formed team to expedite jet engine production. This was not, of course, the role that Whittle saw for Power Jets, which he naturally believed should be taking the lead role in any new jet engine production venture. Although he was somewhat in awe of Freeman, who like Whittle had started out as a pilot officer and then had a very distinguished RAF career, Whittle could not bring himself to agree with the proposal to put Rolls-Royce in charge of all jet engine work and the meeting ended without a clear consensus. It did leave Whittle seriously depressed, however, and seemed to bring all of the challenges facing the future of Power Jets to a head.

Freeman also knew that the Rover team was making slow progress with developing their own version of Whittle's engine, even though they had established their factory at Barnoldswick for production of jet engines. Ernest Hives, the managing director of Rolls-Royce, knew the Wilks brothers, who ran Rover, quite well and in November 1942 he arranged to meet for dinner with Spencer Wilks, the managing director of Rover, in the Swan and Royal hotel in nearby Clitheroe. During this meeting he was accompanied by a young Stanley Hooker, who much later on became managing director of Rolls-Royce, and then famously came out of retirement to lead the company out of bankruptcy following its collapse in 1971.

After dinner Hives suggested bluntly to Wilks that Rover was not making much progress with the jet development and did not seem to really have their heart in it. He suggested that Rolls-Royce, who were already the largest manufacturer of conventional aero engines, were much better placed to push the jet engine ahead. Hives then offered to swap the Rolls-Royce tank engine factory in Nottingham for the Rover jet engine factory in Barnoldswick. Wilks, who by then was quite frustrated with the slow progress that his team was making with the jet engine, readily agreed to a straight swap with no money changing hands. Hives, of course, realised that the demand for tank engines would be severely reduced following the war, although this did not seem to affect Wilks's decision to get out of the jet engine business. This turned out to be a momentous event for Rolls-Royce, however, and for the future of the jet engine. Today, and despite the financial collapse in 1971 and eventual resurrection of the company, Rolls-Royce is one of the largest manufacturers of jet engines in the world.

At the end of a meeting on 12 December 1942 to finalise plans for the takeover of Rover jet engine production by Rolls-Royce, Whittle had a brief meeting alone with Hives. When Hives asked Whittle how he felt about the developments going forward, Whittle replied somewhat tellingly by saying, 'I told him that I was much more enthusiastic about the proposals than I had appeared to be. It was difficult for me to appear enthusiastic about anything in my present state of health.'[50] He was clearly devastated by the prospect of losing control of his brilliant new engine, and this was having a very negative effect on his state of mind. Whittle was, of course, fully aware of the enormous capabilities of Rolls-Royce, the luxury car company that had evolved and expanded to become the largest designers and manufacturers of aircraft piston engines, including the ubiquitous Merlin V-12 engine that powered most of the then current crop of warplanes. He realised, therefore, that once Rolls-Royce got involved with the design and manufacturing of jet engines, it really meant the end of his dream of having Power Jets become the main supplier of his radical new propulsion system.

Stanley Hooker, who Hives increasingly relied upon for his judgement and expertise in research and development, took Whittle aside after a meeting to finalise plans for the takeover by Rolls-Royce and said, 'Frank, you must realise that now that Rolls-Royce have taken over and intend to put their full weight behind your engine, the control of the engine must necessarily pass to us. With the facilities at our disposal, it is no use you trying to compete. On the contrary, you must join with us, and give us the benefit of your talents and experience. We will march forward together, me as your man, only too anxious to have direction and advice from you.'[51]

Hooker realised that this must have been a very painful moment for Whittle, and was impressed by his unselfishness when he readily agreed to this suggestion. From then on, Whittle left most of the detailed design and manufacturing decisions to Hooker and his team at Rolls-Royce, while he continued to work with his small team at Power Jets on further developments of the engine in order to increase its power and reliability. Whittle and Hooker also became close friends in later life, with each man having great admiration and respect for the other.

Whittle and his Power Jets team at the new Whetstone facilities continued to work on variants of the W2B engine, which had shown promise in the Meteor fighter. During his absence in the United States Whittle's team had rapidly finished the design of the W2/500 engine, which was a further development of the W2B. This engine was successfully run just a month after Whittle's return from America, and in a short time on the test bench reached its design performance objectives with a thrust of 1,750lb. Although Whittle and the Power Jets team hoped that this would prove to be their entry into mass production, the much larger design and development team working at Rolls-Royce were going flat out to build their production version of the W2B, which they called the Welland, to power the Meteor. The Power Jets team were also working on a further development of the W2/500 with an increase in thrust to 2,000lb and designated the W2/700. However, Rolls-Royce were making rapid progress in further development of their Welland design, which ultimately achieved the same 2,000lb of thrust. This essentially ended the role that Power Jets would play in developing production versions of Whittle's jet engine. When Rolls-Royce took over the Rover factory in Barnoldswick at the beginning of 1943, the move also incorporated a small design office that Rover had established in nearby Clitheroe. The chief designer there was Adrian Lombard, who along with many other staff had joined the Rolls-Royce team. Lombard was an outstanding design engineer and ended up being chief engineer at Rolls-Royce. Although the Rolls-Royce headquarters is now in Derby, and much of the manufacturing takes place there, the Barnoldswick plant continues to be one of their main factories. It also provides the genesis of the naming of many Rolls-Royce jet engines beginning with 'RB' (eg. RB211), which stands for Rolls-Royce Barnoldswick.

In early 1943 Winston Churchill visited Power Jets and met Whittle and his team. This was clearly an important event for Whittle, and the Power Jets team seemed pleased with the Prime Minister's very positive reaction to seeing the E.28/39 in flight. This was clearly an important moment for Whittle and the Power Jets team, and they seemed to feel that more government funding would likely be available to commercialise jet engine production. During the first few months of 1943 Whittle and his Power Jets founding partners, Tinling and Johnson, turned their attention to trying to develop some form of commercial linkage between Power Jets and Rolls-Royce. They could foresee that following the war there would likely be a large commercial demand for the new jet engine, and naturally wanted to be in a position to benefit from this. They wrote several letters to Rolls-Royce in which they suggested either a merger of the two companies, or some type of licensing arrangement for the patents that had been obtained by Power Jets. However, given the fact that Power Jets had been funded by the government for most of their development work, the legal right to enforce their patents in wartime was not clear. Whittle was also very much concerned about the long-term funding for Power Jets, and proposed to Stafford Cripps, the Minister of Aircraft Production, nationalisation of the complete emerging gas turbine and jet engine industry. Unfortunately, a few months later Cripps told Whittle that he intended to just nationalise Power Jets.

Rolls-Royce, of course, was a very large and powerful company, and was able to effectively ignore any claim by Power Jets for compensation related to patents that had been effectively funded with public money during the war. In the end, Rolls-Royce, as the much larger and better-funded firm, was able to stall any obligations they may have to compensate Power Jets for Whittle's original patents, while continuing to file patents for their own modifications to his original design. They were also clearly looking to supply the large demand for non-military jet engines that they could envisage coming following the end of hostilities. The fact that they appeared to be deliberately avoiding any commercial tie-up between the two companies naturally seemed to be very unfair to Whittle and his co-founders. Towards the end of 1943 Cripps confirmed that he would be nationalising Power Jets, and would pay no more than £100,000 for the company. This situation, of course, did nothing to help the state of Whittle's increasingly fragile mental health.

This period really marked the beginning of the end for Whittle's direct control over the design and manufacturing of jet engines, and he found this very difficult to accept. He had put so much of his life into development of the engine and had overcome so many obstacles along the way that it was naturally very painful to see it essentially snatched away from him just as it was becoming a revolutionary new source of propulsion. He began to realise, of course, that the commercial development of the novel engine he had worked so hard to develop would be largely undertaken by others. As a result, he never really recovered his equilibrium and suffered from stress and mental health issues for the next few years. As he was no longer completely immersed in designing new versions and variations of the jet engine, or in directly supervising the manufacturing and testing of engines, Whittle decided that he needed to concentrate on his career as an RAF officer. As a result, in May 1943 he was sent off to the RAF Staff College in Buckinghamshire for a three-month war course. This provided a much-needed change for a man who had been under great strain trying to get his jet engine into commercial production.

He enjoyed having the opportunity to do some flying again, and was also very pleased to be promoted to the rank of group captain.

Meanwhile, Tinling and Johnson were trying to think of ways in which Power Jets, and its shareholders, could monetise their many years of hard work in trying to bring Whittle's invention to commercial fruition. In early June 1943, Tinling wrote to Roxbee Cox in an effort to lay out the Power Jets case for benefitting from jet engine production following the war.[52] Tinling outlined several specific proposals that would compensate Power Jets shareholders from future commercial production of the new engine and reward the original investors for the risk they had taken:

1. All manufacturers would pay the Treasury a 5 per cent royalty on the revenues from all jet engines built in a ten-year period after the War.
2. The Government would build up the strongest possible case to have similar arrangements with foreign manufacturers anywhere in the world.
3. The Government would award Power Jets 20 per cent of the fund so created. (As a shareholder, the Government would then have 20 per cent or so of this payment returned to it.)
4. The net effect would be a Royalty payment to Power Jets private shareholders of 0.8 per cent of the revenue from all jet engines built, with the remaining 4.2 per cent going to the public purse.

Tinling finished his letter by saying, 'You will appreciate that this is a scheme; it has not the formal approval of my Board, still less the necessary vote of shareholders to implement it. It is sent to you as an invitation to comment and for discussion. Please note that this scheme is not exclusive of any other current proposal.'

However, there doesn't appear to be any further correspondence related to this rather brash proposal, and no action seems to have been taken on the specific proposals suggested. It also seems likely that the proposal from Tinling had not been seen by Whittle, who was still on his training course at the RAF Staff College at the time.

This period also coincided with the first flight of the Gloster Meteor, the very first operational jet fighter aircraft. Design work on this ground-breaking aeroplane had begun in 1936 after it had become clear that Whittle's new engine would be likely to supersede the then ubiquitous Rolls-Royce Merlin piston engine that powered most of the RAF aircraft then in production. The Meteor first flew on 5 March 1943, powered by two Rolls-Royce Welland engines, which had been designed in close collaboration with Whittle under the licence arrangement with Power Jets. The aircraft proved to be a very successful fighter, and at the time was the fastest aeroplane in existence with a top speed exceeding 400mph (640km/h). It entered service in July 1944 and did not have the same impact on the outcome of the war as the ubiquitous Hurricane and Spitfire, although it became the standard fighter in the RAF and many other air forces after the war.

Chapter 9

Nationalisation

A week after Tinling's letter to Roxbee Cox, Whittle wrote to Sir Stafford Cripps, the Minister of Aircraft Production, to suggest quite another approach to the compensation of Power Jets shareholders for their role in developing a commercially viable jet engine. He enclosed a brief document that outlined his estimation of the overall value of the assets of Power Jets, which he put at £810,000.[53] By far the largest item in this list was the assumed value of foreign patent rights, which he assumed to be worth £500,000. Other items included his estimation of 'the moral obligation of the state to the company', valued at £100,000, as well as 'the value of the team in being', estimated at £50,000. Whittle suggested that Power Jets should be nationalised, and shareholders should be paid a lump sum of £500,000, which would compensate them for their initial risk in funding the company.[54] He also said, 'The views I hold are such that it is extremely distasteful to have to recommend such a figure, but my desire to see a clean-cut transfer from private to public ownership is so great that I think it is worth it.' This letter underlies Whittle's socialist leanings at the time, which led him to see the future of the company he created becoming equivalent to other nationalised industries, such as British Rail.

It seems that this letter was accepted at face value by Cripps, who would ultimately nationalise Power Jets. However, rather than turning it into a state-owned manufacturing company, he decided that it should become a national research organisation, rather than a design and production company. This then left the field wide open for large commercial enterprises, such as Rolls-Royce and General Electric in the US, to benefit from the production of jet engines for both military and civilian aviation.

The new Power Jets facilities at Whetstone were a huge improvement over those at the original cramped site in Lutterworth, and initially Whittle thought that they would be suitable for production as well as for research and development. He soon realised, however, that large-scale manufacturing would be dominated by companies such as Rolls-Royce, even though they had not provided the critical intellectual property upon which the engine was based. He also realised that the government had put a great deal of money into the early development of the engine, and as a lifelong socialist he felt that the state should benefit from doing so as much, or even more, than purely commercial interests. He believed, however, that nationalisation would ensure that the relatively small Power Jets staff would be part of a new organisation that would not be completely dominated by large industrial companies such as Rolls-Royce and the other companies now starting to work on jet development.

He later came to regret writing the letter to Cripps, who, as a member of the Labour party, was quite happy to consider Whittle's proposal. The result, however, was that Power Jets was nationalised and turned into a government research and development laboratory, while Rolls-Royce and others were free to make as much profit as possible from manufacturing jet engines.

In Whittle's absence Tinling and Dudley-Williams were left to negotiate terms with the Ministry of Aircraft Production for closing down Power Jets and turning it into a state-owned research and development centre. This new government venture would end up relying on contracts from firms such as Rolls-Royce to carry out basic research, rather than designing new engines. After nationalisation the Whetstone facilities built especially for Power Jets were brought together with the RAE turbine division at Pyestock, near Farnborough in Hampshire, becoming Power Jets (R&D) Ltd. Morale was poor in the new research-orientated Power Jets, and many of the staff who were loyal to Whittle left, with some going to Rolls-Royce or one of the other aero engine companies now joining the race to commercialise this radical new form of propulsion. Whittle had already suggested that he would give his shares in Power Jets to the Ministry as he believed this was the duty of a serving officer. In the final iteration for the company, the facilities at Whetstone, together with the former RAE facilities at Pyestock, were moved into a new and larger establishment on the Pyestock site. The combined facilities were then renamed the National Gas Turbine Establishment (NGTE) in 1948, and continued to conduct basic research on jet engines and other forms of gas turbines until finally closing in 2000. This move finally recognised that the development of jet engines and gas turbines in the future would be undertaken primarily by large companies, dominated by Rolls-Royce in the UK and by GE and Pratt & Whitney in the US. Whittle stayed on as an 'advisor' to the new research organisation, but in reality he spent little time there and worked to rebuild his RAF career.

By the end of 1943, with the jet engine now a proven commodity, there was considerable uncertainty about how a whole new industry should be developed to take advantage of Whittle's early work on his revolutionary engine. Whittle was involved in many discussions with government officials about the role of Power Jets and other companies going forward with commercial development. It became quite clear that the Labour government were determined to nationalise Power Jets, a move that Whittle originally supported. However, he also believed that the other companies now involved in designing and building jet engines should also be nationalised, which he believed the Labour government might support.

During a visit over the New Year holiday, Dr Guy of the MAP asked Whittle how he felt about the possible nationalisation of Power

Jets. As he still had socialist leanings, Whittle replied that he was in favour of nationalising the gas turbine engine industry as a whole, but he was very dubious of nationalising just Power Jets on its own.[55] The reality, however, was that the large manufacturing firms were far too powerful and influential to succumb to a government takeover, with the end result that only Power Jets was nationalised. Whittle felt very let down by this, but eventually came to accept that the large commercially minded companies were best placed to take jet engine production forward on a truly international scale.

At the beginning of 1944 Whittle was awarded the CBE (Commander of the British Empire) in the New Year Honours list. He was naturally very pleased to be recognised in this way, as it was something a young man with his humble background would not normally even dream of.

During this time Whittle also met Cripps again. Whittle asked whether the gas turbine industry as a whole might be nationalised. Cripps replied that he 'had given up hope on this, as the political situation just did not permit it'.[56] Whittle replied that he was very disappointed to hear that, and the discussion went on to what was to become of Power Jets, into which so much government money had been invested. Cripps indicated that it was likely that Power Jets itself might be nationalised, becoming a national research institute for all forms of gas turbines, rather than a manufacturing entity. Whittle seemed to be resigned to this outcome, and Cripps told him that he wanted Power Jets to get all the credit it deserved for its achievements. The conversation then turned to the composition of a Board of Directors for the new research institute, and Cripps said that he hoped that Whittle would be willing to be a director. Whittle replied that he would be but only if he was not required to give up his position in the RAF.

As a result, Roxbee Cox became chairman and managing director of Power Jets, and said that, 'I was Whittle's entrepreneur.' The discussion then concluded with Cripps asking him if the price of £130,000 being proposed to buy all the outstanding Power Jets shares was 'fair'. Whittle said that he did not really know, but he was disappointed that it had just been imposed on the company under the threat of a 'big stick'. Cripps replied by saying that the Ministry had been successful in getting a big increase from the £100,000 that the Treasury had been proposing. The meeting then finished with Cripps asking Whittle if the offer he had made, as a serving RAF officer, to tender his shares to the Ministry, still stood. When Whittle replied that it did, the Minister told him it would not make any difference to the total price paid for the company, but that Whittle's decision to give up his shares would make them more valuable to the remaining shareholders. Three days after this meeting with the Minister, Whittle telephoned Roxbee Cox at the MAP to discuss the transfer of Power Jets into public ownership.[57] Roxbee Cox expressed surprise at Whittle's offer to give up his shares, and asked why he had done it. Whittle replied that he believed it was his duty to do so, although he did not like doing it, particularly as it would only increase the amount the other shareholders would get.

In early 1944 both the British and US governments realised that there should be some kind of public acknowledgement of the revolutionary new propulsion system that had been pioneered by Whittle and his team. Although Whittle had been made aware by government officials that there would soon be some kind of announcement, he was not told of the timing. He was rather surprised, therefore, when late on 6 January 1944, he was handed an early copy of the next day's *Daily Herald* newspaper, which would tell the world of the successful development of the jet engine. The next morning he would wake up to find his achievements trumpeted on the front page of every major national newspaper. The front page of the *Daily Express*, for example, had a photo of Whittle working with his slide rule, and the headline 'Britain has Fighter with no Propeller', and the somewhat amusing subheading 'Driven by Hot Air' (see Plate 16). Whittle's family was also the subject of some of the publicity in the press, with the headline in one paper exclaiming 'Inventor's wife kept secret for 14 years'. She was quoted as saying that, 'For 14 years, since before we were married, I have lived with this secret of the propeller-less plane.' She went on to say, 'I suppose now that the secret is out, my husband will start on another idea. He thinks years ahead.' The article also quoted Whittle's 9-year-old son, Ian, who said that, 'It's the kind of plane I'm going to pilot when I grow up.' 'And, true to his conviction, Ian would go on to be a senior captain with British Airways. His older brother, David, who was 12 at the time, was also quoted two days later in the *News Chronicle*, saying that his father didn't usually play with them when he got home. He said, however, 'I can talk to him about mechanical things, and he will tell me where I have gone wrong with the models I have been making. But my father has no time for model making. He is just too tired.' Whittle's long-time friend and close colleague Johnny Johnson, was quoted in the *Daily Mail* as saying 'this unswerving belief in his own peculiar powers of analysis is perhaps the dominating factor which has led to the present outcome'.

Being a very private person, and quite shy at the best of times, Whittle found it very trying to be bombarded by the press for several days and to be the recipient of endless queries about his revolutionary new engine. He said, 'I was by no means prepared for the astonishing consequences of publication. I had been too close to the job for many years to see the situation from the point of view of the average citizen. Our failures were more prominent in my mind than our successes, and so the reaction of the Press and the public had a stunning effect.'[58]

Just four days after the press announcement, Whittle wrote to the Minister of Aircraft Production, Stafford Cripps, to inform him that he would be giving up all of his shares in Power Jets. Roxbee

Cox gave an address to the employees of Power Jets, telling them of Whittle's selfless act. Whittle confirmed his decision to do so on several occasions, and was then encouraged by many of his colleagues to apply to the Royal Commission on Awards to Inventors, which had been established for just such a situation. Whittle's pride prevented him from doing so, however, and he continued to maintain that he had just been doing his duty as a serving officer in the RAF.

At the beginning of March 1944, Whittle and his wife were invited to a reception at Buckingham Palace, where they met King George VI and Queen Elizabeth.[59] After mingling for some time with the other guests, Whittle was taken by an equerry to meet the King, who spent some time questioning him about the new engine. The King had obviously been briefed quite well before meeting Whittle, and his first question was whether it was possible to bring the fuel consumption down. This naturally surprised Whittle somewhat, but he was pleasantly surprised by the King's interest. Whittle told him that it wasn't a huge problem, and that the new jet fighter was able to stay in the air for the same length of time as a Spitfire. The King then expressed his interest in seeing the new jet-propelled aeroplane fly, and Whittle told him of demonstration flights that were being proposed at Hatfield, not too far from London. The King finished the conversation by asking if the new engine would be of any use for civil aviation. When Whittle replied that it would completely revolutionise all of aviation, the King seemed to be surprised. At the end of the conversation the King turned to Whittle's wife and asked if she had helped in any way. When she said that she was afraid that she hadn't, the King replied, 'Of course you have.'

The process of winding up Power Jets and the dispersal of staff to other companies and the new research facilities at Pyestock was very painful for Whittle, who realised that he had now lost control of the commercial development of his revolutionary new engine. As a result he was hospitalised for 'exhaustion' and a severe case of eczema in his ears. He was likely suffering from what would now be recognised as a deep depression. His stay in Princess Mary's RAF hospital at Halton, near Aylesbury, lasted for five months, from 20 March 1944 to the end of August that year, with a brief period in the RAF officers' hospital, Cleveleys, in Blackpool.

During his time in hospital the Normandy landings took place in June 1944, which was the beginning of the end of the war. Whittle was naturally pleased to learn that the first Meteors, each powered by two Rolls-Royce Welland jet engines, would enter service in July. The first in service were used to chase and shoot down V-1 'flying bombs' that were proving to be a real threat to London. The jet-propelled Meteors had a distinct speed advantage over all piston-engined aircraft, which made them ideally suited for this important task. One pilot, on finding his guns jammed, pulled alongside a flying bomb and then used its wing to tip the wing of the V-1 and force it to crash.

Whittle's lengthy stay in hospital was no doubt partly due to physical exhaustion after several years of single-minded devotion to bringing his new engine to life, and was also likely due to feeling that all of his dedication had not provided the financial security that he had hoped to have for his family. Having promised to give his shares to the MAP, he likely believed that it was unfair that he was the only one of the original team to not benefit in any way financially from his ground-breaking invention. Just after entering hospital at the end of March he received a letter from Cripps, who wrote:[60]

> I have just learned that the formal agreements, under which you are transferring to the State without payment all your financial interest in Power Jets Ltd., have been signed.
>
> Now that this transaction is complete I want to tell you how greatly I appreciate the high conception of your duty which had led you to make this gift to the State, and to tender you my sincere thanks for your generous action.

May I also take this opportunity of expressing my admiration of the inventive genius and hard work you have put into the development of your engine? It represents a valuable asset to the State and the success already achieved must be as gratifying to you as it is to me.

Yours sincerely

Stafford Cripps

This letter came as a surprise to Whittle, and was likely comforting during his lengthy stay in hospital. He sent a brief reply, in which he said:[61]

As you know, it is not without a very considerable wrench that I have done what I have, but my peace of mind is much greater now that the thing is over and done with. The more I think about it the more sure I am that there was no other course open to me.

While he was in hospital, a special meeting of Power Jets shareholders was held to debate just one resolution, 'That the Company be wound up voluntarily'. The motion was then duly approved with a vote of six for and two against. This vote, by just eight people, effectively marked the end of Whittle's dream of his company changing the world.

After he left hospital at the end of August, Whittle did not receive another formal RAF posting. He was very pleased, however, to receive a letter from Air Marshal Ralph Sorley telling him that he was being promoted to acting air commodore. This rank is equivalent to that of brigadier in the British Army, or a one-star general in US terms. Sadly, this also marked the end of his direct involvement with the revolutionary new form of propulsion that he had invented and developed to the point of demonstrating its ultimate role in powering all future forms of military and civil aviation.

At Roxbee Cox's urging, however, he agreed to join the board of directors of the 'new' Power Jets (R&D) Ltd. company. Hayne Constant, the former Imperial College academic, was appointed as the Director of Research and Development. Whittle continued to maintain his office in Brownsover Hall, and from there he would provide as much input as he could to the detailed design and development work now being carried out at the new Whetstone facilities.

At this time, however, it was also becoming clear to Whittle and others, that Rolls-Royce were really moving quickly to become a dominant player in the new jet engine field. At the beginning of December 1944, Whittle received a lengthy letter from Stanley Hooker, now leading the development of jet engines at the company.[62] Hooker reported on a meeting with the MAP in which he said that the Ministry had said it believed that in the future all 'interceptor fighter' aircraft would be powered by jet engines. He discussed the possibility of new jet-engined heavy bombers which would potentially fly much higher than the then-current piston engine-powered aircraft. He also suggested that Rolls-Royce were looking at the possibility of developing jet engines for these using the new 'ducted fan' jet engine design being developed by Dr Alan Arnold Griffith at the Royal Aircraft Establishment. Griffith had for some time been contemplating the use of gas turbine engines to drive a conventional propeller, which was the basis of modern 'turboprop' engines. The 'ducted fan' approach, in which the 'propeller' is essentially the first stage of the engine embedded in the outer nacelle, is now the mainstay of all modern large-scale jet engines.

The original intention for the new Power Jets (R&D) Company was to focus on research and development, which would include the manufacturing of 'small batches' of test engines. In hindsight, with Rolls-Royce then going flat out to manufacture their version of the new engine, this seems like an inappropriate mandate for the new Crown corporation. Also, Whittle found that his new 'advisory' role in the new company was not what he was used to, which he found very frustrating. He evidently felt that Roxbee Cox had lost confidence in him and that he should really leave the company. On one occasion he protested a decision by the new company management, saying, 'I do not accept that when I am in a minority on engineering matters that this means that I am wrong.' He also told Roxbee Cox that he 'would not accept the position in which Constant's judgement is held to rank with mine in the gas turbine field'.

At the beginning of March 1945, Roxbee Cox visited the new Power Jets (R&D) facilities and told the assembled employees that the new jet-powered Meteor fighters 'had been in action'. He also told them that Whittle had been 'unwell for much of last year'.

Shortly after this meeting, Whittle was very pleased to receive a letter from the MAP informing him that the Royal Commission on Awards to Inventors had decided to provide him with an 'interim payment' of £10,000 (equal to about £440,000 today). He was also told that this payment would not prejudice the eventual decision by the Royal Commission.

Whittle's hopes of Power Jets becoming a major manufacturer of his new jet engine were further diminished at a meeting of the recently established Gas Turbine Technical Advisory and Co-ordinating Committee held on 18 April 1945. Whittle was not present at this meeting, which was comprised mainly of senior members of the large aero engine companies, including Ernest Hives from Rolls-Royce and Frank Halford from De Havilland. The meeting minutes indicated that if Power Jets designed and built engines they would be in competition with industry. The minutes concluded that 'what would be satisfactory would be a purely research-minded Power Jets'.

A week after this meeting took place, the board of directors of Power Jets (R&D) Ltd met to discuss the industry views on 'competition'. The following morning Whittle resigned from the Gas Turbine committee. With the end of the war in Europe declared on 8 May 1945, the future of jet engine development was now clearly in the hands of the large aero engine manufacturers, such as Rolls-Royce in the UK and GE in the USA.

Chapter 10

Post-War Developments

Just after the war in Europe was officially declared over, the new Power Jets research centre at Whetstone held a celebratory fete on Saturday, 21 July 1945 for its employees and their families. This included a fly past of a Meteor over the Whetstone show ground in order to showcase the performance of its two jet engines. The Meteor had been assigned by the RAF to Power Jets as a test bed for evaluating the new 'reheat' system of its RB37 engines supplied by Rolls-Royce. The aeroplane was piloted by Squadron Leader Alan Moffet, the chief test pilot assigned by the RAF to the newly established Whetstone research centre. The Meteor approached the nearby Whetstone airfield at an altitude of only 500ft while travelling at nearly 450 knots. It then pulled up steeply into cloud and was next seen levelling out inverted just before diving into the ground at nearby Halls Farm, disintegrating completely. This naturally came as a great shock to all of the family and friends of the Power Jets employees, as well as to Whittle and his fellow jet engine pioneers. The Meteor hit the ground at a very high speed, and the damage was such that the post-accident investigation could find no particular reason for the loss of control and crash of the aircraft.

In late 1945, Whittle finally got the opportunity to fly an aeroplane powered by his radical new engine design. On 1 October, he was visiting RAF Manston, where Meteors were then being flown. There seems to have been some concern that he wasn't really qualified at the time to fly the new twin-engine fighter, but fellow officers clearly turned a blind eye as they watched him climb into the cockpit of a

Meteor at the end of a day of test flights that he had been watching. He was thrilled, however, to be able to take off in the fighter, which had been so useful towards the end of the war. However, a week after the flight, he wrote a somewhat apologetic letter to Air Marshal Cryton, who was Controller of Research and Development in the Ministry of Aircraft Production. He indicated that there had been no particular plan for him to fly the Meteor, but that he was lucky to be present just at the end of the day's official flying schedule and had not really been told that he should not try to fly the new aeroplane.

At the beginning of 1946, Whittle, who had been appointed to the board of directors of the 'new' Power Jets research establishment, wrote to Roxbee Cox, who was now the chairman and managing director of Power Jets (R&D) Ltd, to express his great concern for the future of the company and to offer his resignation from the board. In his long letter Whittle said that he could no longer support the mission of the new company, which essentially had been transformed to provide support to the established aero engine companies, such as Rolls-Royce, De Havilland and Metropolitan Vickers. In part he said that:[63]

> It is with much regret that I must ask you to accept my resignation from the Board of Power Jets (R&D) Ltd. I am very sorry indeed to have to take this step, but I have come to the conclusion that I can no longer share the responsibility for the affairs of the company in circumstances unfavourable to constructive effort, however able the members of the Board may be.
>
> The primary factor in the whole unfortunate situation is that the Power Jets engineering team is largely built up of engineers who have an intense interest in doing a practical job of work, who desire to see their products used, who are only interested in research as a necessary ancillary to development

and not as an end in itself, and who require the stimulus of a succession of fruitful short-term objectives. In short, the team is not suited to the present functions of the company. It is the right crew in the wrong ship. They feel that things have gone from bad to worse since 1940. Before the company was nationalised there was strong resentment against the restriction of functions of the old Power Jets to research and development. The team – the pioneers who had launched the aircraft gas turbine – regarded this as a grave injustice. Not only did they believe that their pioneer status entitled them to be provided with all the necessary facilities to carry the job through, but they also believed, rightly, that they were the most competent designers, which also entitled them to those facilities. Instead they were restricted to research and development, were compelled to hand over their techniques to other firms, and had the mortification of seeing these other firms given a licence in design for which they were not qualified, and provided with facilities far greater than themselves.

The company has lost all real initiative. It does not own the capital equipment it uses, nor any funds with which work can be initiated at the sole discretion of the Board. It may not start an engine project without first receiving a contract from the MAP, and these contracts are rarely forthcoming. When, after much labour, a carefully considered proposal is submitted it gets a lukewarm reception. We are told that it is the wrong size, or that it is not ambitious, that it is our duty to be 'two jumps ahead' of anybody else. In other words, we are expected to make an immense detour into desert regions where there is no practical stimulation to refresh the traveller. Moreover, certain Ministry officials who have never been responsible for the design of a gas turbine, and for whose technical competence our engineers have very little respect, show a strong tendency to dictate the programme of work in the company. In short the team finds itself with far less scope for initiative than it possessed many years ago when the available facilities were very meagre. It is dominated both technically and financially by the MAP.

Whittle finished up his three-page letter by saying:

I find myself in sympathy with the views of the majority of the engineers and therefore do not regard myself as suited to head the engineering team of a research and development organisation of the type Power Jets is supposed to be. My forte is to direct a few large-scale projects toward a near and worthwhile objective. I cannot arouse much interest in a myriad of small-scale and relatively unrelated experiments which end merely in a mass of reports.

This letter really ended Whittle's active involvement in steering the development of new versions of his ground-breaking invention, and it was no doubt a very bitter pill for him to swallow. From that point forward he had little direct involvement in the design and development of the new crop of jet engines being designed and developed by several major firms both in the UK and the USA. His no-doubt painful departure from the company he single-handedly built up also spurred on the resignation in solidarity of sixteen key Power Jets employees. Although most of these would go on to find employment with the larger firms that were then building jet engines, including Rolls-Royce and De Havilland, Whittle no doubt felt some solace in their clear message of solidarity with him. In replying to a letter to Rolls-Royce from one of the disgruntled Power Jets employees, Stanley Hooker replied, 'To me, whatever shape or form these engines take, they will always remain Whittle engines.'[64]

In early June 1946, Whittle received a letter from the Ministry of Supply, confirming his appointment as Technical Advisor on Engine Design. This appointment was to be for two years, and he would retain the rank of air commodore. The letter also noted that 'the Minister is glad to know that you will be undertaking the American tour, as arranged'. This was just to confirm the arrangements made by the Ministry of Supply for Whittle to give a series of lectures and presentations on jet engine design and development in the USA. It turned out to be a lengthy trip, as he left England on 16 June 1946 and did not return until 10 September. He readily agreed to make the journey, however, and ended up visiting eighteen different cities around the country.

In addition to the lectures, Whittle was asked to visit many different companies and factories, and to provide his opinion on a wide array of jet engine-related research now being ramped up in the US. This was a very full schedule, and Whittle was very pleased to be provided with secretarial support from the British Women's Auxiliary Air Force (WAAF) by the assignment of S/O (Section Officer) Jane Shepherd to accompany him. In a brief description of her posting, Ms Shepherd said that other secretaries she met during the tour, 'all envied me my opportunities of travelling round the country rather than sitting in an office as they did. I fully realised how very lucky I was to have the chance I did. The whole trip was a wonderful experience which I will always remember with pleasure as the most exciting event in my WAAF career.'[65] Although he was by then very weary from working non-stop on development of his engine, Whittle was able to complete his tour of the US and even found the energy to give a lecture in Paris on the way home in early September 1946.

Although his first lecture tour had been a great success, it was probably unwise of Whittle to agree, only a month later, to return to the US again to conduct a second such tour. He once more travelled across the country giving lectures, and receiving a number of awards, including the prestigious US Legion of Merit in Washington DC, and the Guggenheim medal awarded by the American Society of Mechanical Engineers.

This time, however, he found the hectic schedule to be too much, and he decided to travel to Bermuda for a month of rest and relaxation. In January 1947 he returned to the US to continue his lecture tour, but again found the strain to be so great that he ended up in the US Naval Hospital in Bethesda, Maryland (now known as the Walter Reed National Military Medical Center). He remained in hospital there for the next three months suffering from nervous exhaustion, finally returning to England at the end of March.

During his stay in hospital this time he met another patient who was to have a significant role much later in his life. Her name was Hazel Steenberg, a US Navy nurse who had contracted a tropical disease while working with patients who were exposed to a number of unknown diseases while serving in the tropics. Ms Steenberg was universally known as 'Tommie', a nickname she was given as a very young girl when she tried giving herself a haircut with a pair of scissors. When her father first saw her he asked if there was a new boy in the house, and if he might be called 'Tom'.[66] The diminutive form, Tommie, then quickly became the nickname by which she was known within the family from then on. Before joining the navy in 1943 she had worked as a stewardess for TWA at a time when flight attendants (as they are now called) were required to have a nursing background. Perhaps because of her extensive flying experience, she enjoyed chatting with Whittle during their free time in the hospital.

After finally being discharged from the hospital Whittle gave some lectures in Canada, and then returned to England. He kept in touch with Tommie after leaving the hospital, however, and they would often arrange to meet on the many subsequent occasions when Whittle visited the US.

Unfortunately, shortly after returning to England Whittle's health again deteriorated and he once more ended up in hospital until late 1947. Early in the new year of 1948 he realised that retirement from the RAF was most likely the best course of action. After some discussions with senior RAF officials, including Lord Tedder, now the Chief of the Air Staff, it was agreed that Whittle would retire with the rank of air commodore. Whittle was quite satisfied with this, and found that his pension plus a temporary post in the Ministry of Supply left his financial situation relatively unchanged. This was to be only a short-term appointment, however, as in May 1948 he learned that the Royal Commission on Awards to Inventors had recommended that he be awarded a tax-free sum of £100,000, equivalent to approximately £4,500,000, or nearly $5,700,000, in today's terms. This would be the largest award made to any inventor from the war years. The very substantial award was likely in large part due to the glowing letter of support sent to the Royal Commission by Roxbee Cox (later to become Lord Kings Norton), who, as chairman of the Gas Turbine Collaboration Committee, had worked closely with Whittle during the later stages of development of the jet engine. In part the letter read:

> Whittle's contribution was the association of jet propulsion and the gas turbine. Before him the gas turbine had been regarded, like other turbines, as a machine for supplying shaft power. Whittle recognised it as the ideal means of providing jet propulsion for aircraft. It is one thing to have an idea. It is another to have the technical and executive ability to give it flesh. It is still another to have the tenacity of purpose to drive through to success unshaken in confidence, in the face of discouraging opposition. Whittle, whose name in the annals of engineering comes after those of Watt, Stephenson and Parsons only for reasons of chronology or alphabetical order,

had these things. It may be said that without Whittle the jet propulsion engine and the other applications of the gas turbine would have come just the same. They would. But they would have come much later. Whittle's work gave this country a technical lead of at least two years. So far the gas turbine has been generally regarded as a means of propulsion of fighting aircraft. I think posterity will see it rather as a great commercial asset – presuming that we today do our duty in exploiting it. They will see too that the initiative in its development came from aeronautical technologists, and at the head of them they will see Whittle.[67]

This award was given to Whittle in recognition of his unique contribution to the future of aviation and his unstinting dedication in turning his brilliant vision into practice.

Needless to say, this dramatic improvement in Whittle's financial situation was a great relief to him, and enabled him to live the rest of his days without worrying about finances. Whittle's brief, but heartfelt, letter to Sir Archibald Rowlands, the permanent secretary to the Ministry of Supply at the time, illustrates how much the recognition meant to him. He wrote in full:

I am overwhelmed by the delightful news contained in your letter of the 27th May. The amount of the Award substantially exceeds my most optimistic expectations.

It means far more to me than a sum of money. It is a magnificent expression of the Nation's appreciation of my work and its value to me in that sense is beyond measure.

The consideration shown for me by all concerned is something I appreciate very much indeed, and I am particularly grateful that I have not been called upon to plead my own case in any way.

My most sincere thanks to the Minister, yourself, and those of the Ministry's officials who went to such trouble in the preparation of my case.

And, to finally recognise the major contribution he had clearly made to the future of aviation, Whittle was further honoured by King George VI with a Knighthood in July 1948.

For someone from Whittle's humble background this was a truly momentous occasion, and he believed that his many years of unstinting dedication and belief in his ideas had finally been recognised at the highest level. Writing about this occasion he said; 'As the King touched me on each shoulder with the sword, I became the first Old Cranwellian to receive the honour of Knighthood. The satisfaction which this gave me was overshadowed by my regret that I was leaving the Service in which I had served since the age of 16, and which had given me the training which made possible the jet engine.'[68] Sir Frank Whittle, despite all he had accomplished, was still only 41, and believed that he still had much to achieve.

Chapter 11

Civilian Life

It did not take long before Whittle began exploring new business possibilities after his retirement from the RAF. He was, of course, now well-known within the aviation industry, and he began by exploring opportunities that might interest him. One of the first congratulatory letters he received after the announcement of his Knighthood in 1948 was from Whitney Straight, CEO of the British Overseas Airways Corporation (BOAC), the forerunner of British Airways, and at that time one of the major international airlines. Straight was born into a well-off American family who moved to Britain when he was a teenager. He was educated at Trinity College, Cambridge, and while still a student he became a well-known racing car driver. He would go on to become a pilot in the RAF during the war, rising rapidly through the ranks to become an air commodore in 1942. Shortly after the war ended he joined BOAC and quickly rose to become the CEO. In his brief note, Straight said:

> May I be among the many to congratulate you on the honour which has been bestowed on you by the King. No man has made a greater contribution to aviation than yourself, and in the years to come we shall be even more in your debt.
>
> If you are ever around these parts, I should be delighted to have a chat with you, or better still perhaps you will join us at lunch one day.

Whittle immediately followed up on Straight's suggestion, and the two men soon agreed that Whittle should serve as an 'honorary advisor' for BOAC. Airlines were beginning to expand rapidly after the war, with new overseas routes opening all the time. Many of the new destinations had inadequate airport facilities for the new larger airliners, and BOAC believed that Whittle might be well suited for visiting potential new destinations for the airline in order to give them some feedback. The airline also likely believed that having such a high-profile figure, as Whittle had become, on their staff would also be very good publicity, which would help to raise their profile. Whittle was given an office, but with only vague instructions on what his role might be in opening new routes for the growing airline. Although his role as honorary advisor did not come with a salary, he was assigned a secretary, Ms Margaret Lawrence, who also acted as his personal assistant. Whittle had been living apart from his family for quite a long time by now, and he decided to live in London, close to the BOAC headquarters. His wife, Dorothy, and two sons, David and Ian, remained behind in Rugby. Whittle was now very well-known in aviation circles, and he was invited to many social events in London. Whittle himself was not very keen on small talk, and he would often take Ms Lawrence to these events to help smooth the conversation. Over time he would end up spending most of his social time with her. He was effectively separated from Dorothy by this time, although they did not formally divorce until 1976.

Whittle travelled to Canada and the US in 1948, with a visit to Vancouver in part to hold discussions with the Boeing Co. which had quite a large operation there at the time. He also met with a group of RCAF (Royal Canadian Air Force) veterans and spoke at their annual meeting on 11 November. He flew from London Heathrow to Montreal on the first leg of this trip in a Trans-Canada Airlines (later to become Air Canada) Canadair North Star. This was a version of the Douglas DC-4 airliner built by Canadair in Montreal that used Rolls-Royce Merlin piston engines in place of the original radials. This made the North Star much faster than the standard DC-4, but also made it a much noisier aeroplane. Whittle remarked that the flight had been very 'tedious and tiring'. While in Vancouver, Whittle had discussions with Trans-Canada Airlines (TCA) and was somewhat surprised to learn that they were much less pessimistic than he was about using jet engines on commercial aircraft.

In his notes of the meeting Whittle said, 'I had the feeling that TCA would in all probability be the first airline to operate civil jet airliners.'[69] In reality, however, TCA's first jet-powered flight did not take place until 1960, when they began using Douglas DC-8 aircraft. These were powered by Rolls-Royce Conway engines, which were the first 'turbofan' engines to enter commercial service. This design, in which the first stage of the compressor was a large-diameter 'fan', resulted in much of the air bypassing the remaining compressor stages as well as the combustion chamber and turbine sections altogether. The turbofan design resulted in higher efficiency and a lower specific fuel consumption compared with a 'straight-through' engine design. All modern airliner engines now incorporate this design, in which the large-diameter fan essentially acts like an enclosed propeller at the front of the engine.

From there he went on to visit the Boeing headquarters in Seattle, where somewhat ironically he was told that Boeing, then building bombers for the US Air Force, had no interest in building commercial airliners.

In early 1949 Whittle would spend several weeks in Epsom, Surrey, not too far from central London. He was staying in a local country club, and took up golfing as a hobby. Much of his time was now spent at the Woodcote Park golf club, which had been established in Coulsdon, not far from Epsom, in 1912. He was well known by now, and spent much of his time there meeting friends and dining in upmarket restaurants not too far away in London, including the Savoy Hotel, with its famous Grill Room. This was not a very familiar lifestyle for someone from Whittle's background, however, and he would soon end up travelling again, and giving lectures about his development of the jet engine.

In early April Whittle attended a meeting of the Reactionaries, a group of more than sixty former Power Jets employees who worked closely with him on the early engine development. The name Reactionaries was a somewhat whimsical term related to Newton's third law, which states that for every action there is an equal and opposite reaction. This group continued to maintain contact for many years, right up until their final meeting in 2001.

During this period Whittle was suffering a number of health-related problems, including 'intercostal neuritis', which is a painful inflammation of nerve tissue. Although not particularly dangerous, it can be a very painful condition that tends to limit movement of the limbs. The discomfort resulting from the infection led to Whittle being somewhat less active than he was used to.

Towards the end of 1949 Whittle and Dorothy viewed a large house, called The Oaks, near Harrow on the Hill, and ended up purchasing it as a family home. Although Dorothy and her sons would enjoy living there, Whittle was travelling constantly and would end up spending very little time there. He also told Whitney Straight that he was giving up Brownsover Hall, and would be moving to Harrow, not far from London airport. His furniture and extensive files were moved out of Brownsover and into a new office at the BOAC headquarters in Brentford, close to what was then called London Airport and now known as Heathrow.

Whittle was now, of course, very well-known and continued to be recognised by many institutions. Towards the end of June 1949, he was awarded an honorary DSc (Doctor of Science) degree from Oxford University. Having not had much formal education, this was a tremendous honour, and was among the first of many awards that would recognise his many accomplishments, despite him having almost no formal higher education. His sons, David and Ian, attended the ceremony at Oxford. Other honourees included Sir Stafford Cripps, now a barrister and diplomat, and Sir John Cockcroft, the well-known scientist who would go on to share the 1951 Nobel Prize in Physics for his role in splitting the atomic nucleus.

In November 1949, Whittle was once again in the US in order to attend the formal unveiling of one of his most important early experimental engines, the W1X, in the Smithsonian Institution in Washington DC. This engine had been run extensively by Power Jets, and was the forerunner of early production engines. During his remarks at the unveiling ceremony Whittle noted that the W1X had been used for taxiing trials of the E.28/39 aeroplane before the subsequent W1 semi-production model was installed for the very first jet-powered flight. He also noted that the W1X was, in effect, the first jet engine to 'fly', as during the taxiing trials the pilot, Gerry Sayer, went fast enough to make one or two 'hops' just off the runway. The W1X was not certified as a flight engine, however, and the first full take-off and test flight was performed with the first 'production engine', just known as the W1. The W1X engine was subsequently sent to the US, where it was used by GE as an example to help in the design of their own jet engine.

In his talk at the Smithsonian Whittle noted that it was very appropriate that the W1X should be deposited there, since it was the very first jet engine to be run in the US. In his final remarks Whittle said, 'I feel very proud indeed of the fact that this engine – for the design of which I was responsible – is being given a permanent place of honour in the United States of America. I like to feel that a part of me has a permanent place over here.'[70] These comments also may have been in part due to the increasing amount of time that Whittle was now spending in the US, and the strengthening of his friendship with Tommie.

Whittle then travelled with Ms Lawrence to visit Nassau and Bermuda, before returning to New York, and then back to England. While in New York, he visited the UK embassy, and told staff there, 'I was convinced that there was a deliberate policy of suppression of references to the British origin of the jet engine. I mentioned the total lack of official invitations in Washington, and the poor news coverage of the W1X presentation ceremony.'

Towards the end of 1949 Whittle received a letter from BOAC CEO Whitney Straight revising his work conditions to now include a personal assistant and two secretaries. Although there was still no mention of pay, he would be allowed to take his wife or his secretary on any BOAC flights. Whittle found travelling to many new destinations in Europe and around the world to be very interesting, and he would always provide a very detailed report of his findings when he returned to London. After some time, however, he believed that his recommendations about possible new routes, and the type of airport facilities required, were not being taken seriously by the senior management at BOAC. Whittle began to suspect that his employment was primarily motivated by the positive publicity that the company received from their association with him, rather than by his technical expertise. He was also unhappy when he was asked to move out of the BOAC executive offices in central London to a new office at Heathrow airport.

At the beginning of 1950 Whittle wrote a note to Whitney Straight, now BOAC deputy chairman, to ask if his extensive travels were still in the best interest of the company. He was reassured by Straight that BOAC were happy to have him continue, because they believed his overseas visits helped to spread goodwill and raise the international profile of the airline. Straight did ask, however, for more details on his expense account. As a result of the reassurances from Straight, Whittle went ahead with a planned tour of India and Pakistan, accompanied by Margaret Lawrence. While there he met a number of local airline officials, and suggested that they should be planning for longer runways in order to accommodate a new generation of jet-propelled aircraft. He argued that these would be of particular benefit to the larger cities such as Bombay and Calcutta. On the way back Whittle and Ms Lawrence spent a few days in Cairo, which was a convenient halfway stop between India and the UK.

After they returned to London, Spencer Wilks invited Whittle to be present at the first trials of a new Rover car powered by one of their gas turbine engines. Whittle refused the offer, however, perhaps because he believed that he had not been sufficiently consulted on the development of Rover's unique turbine-powered car.

On 13 March 1950, Whittle flew for the first time in the new de Havilland Comet, the very first commercial jet-powered aeroplane. Whittle certainly enjoyed his experience, and was invited to take the controls for some time.

Whittle was also beginning to enjoy some of the trappings of being such a highly recognised individual. He had joined the Athenaeum Club, then and now one of the most prestigious members-only social and dining clubs in London. The Athenaeum was opened in 1824, with the object of attracting 'literary and scientific men and followers of the fine arts'. In late March 1950, Whittle noted in his diary that he had lunch with Roxbee Cox during his first visit to the club as a member. He was also now being offered a number of academic posts, including a research chair at the New South Wales University of Technology (now called the University of New South Wales) in Sydney, Australia. Whittle was not really interested in a full-time academic appointment, but he suggested that a lecture tour of Australia might be possible. However, in the end, nothing seemed to come of his suggestion.

Back home in the UK, Whittle was now in demand as a speaker, and was often asked for his thoughts about future jet engine developments. In July 1950, he attended a meeting of the recently established Gas Turbine Collaboration Committee (GTCC) and was asked for his comments about future engine developments. In his talk to the committee he noted that his opposition to axial-flow compressors was 'weakening', although he believed that the then current developments lacked the 'enterprise' of the previous few years of work in this area. In a suggestion that proved to be prescient, he also suggested that much more attention should be given to the development of ducted fans. This type of engine has a large first-stage fan at the front that essentially acts like a conventional propeller. Most of the airflow from this fan bypasses the core of the engine, while the rest of the air passes through the inner compressor stages and the combustor section before exiting the engine. This design of engine, now widely used, is sometimes just referred to as a bypass engine.

Whittle's next visit to North America was from mid-September to mid-October 1950, and this time he crossed the Atlantic Ocean on the mighty RMS *Queen Elizabeth*, the largest and most luxurious ship afloat at the time. Unfortunately, his notes indicate that the ocean crossing had been 'very rough'. During the Canadian portion of this visit he met representatives of the A.V. Roe Canada company (later to be just called Avro Canada), who were working on their ill-fated Arrow Mach 2 jet fighter. The Arrow was powered by a new jet engine, designed by Orenda Engines, also a Canadian company. The Orenda was loosely based on Whittle's early engine design, and was intended to produce 6,500lb of thrust. After discussions with Avro officials, Whittle felt that they were very pessimistic about the prospects for the Orenda, which they told him would likely never enter into mass production. The Arrow first flew in 1958, and although its performance was impressive, in early 1959 the Canadian government cancelled the project, which resulted ultimately in Avro Canada going out of business.

The very first international jet-powered flight took place on 2 May 1952, when a de Havilland Comet operated by BOAC took off from London's Heathrow airport bound for Johannesburg. This new jet airliner was small by today's standards, and transported between thirty-five and forty-five passengers over long distances. Power was provided by four Ghost jet engines, providing 5,000lb of thrust each, which had been developed independently by de Havilland under the leadership of Frank Halford. Later versions featured more powerful Rolls-Royce Avon engines, which provided approximately 7,000lb of thrust each. Although impressive at the time, the power output was modest compared to today's largest engines, which produce over 130,000lb of thrust!

The Comet was also a very modern and futuristic-looking aeroplane, with all four engines neatly embedded in the wings, rather than hung on pylons below them, as in most current commercial aircraft designs. It attracted orders from many other airlines during the early 1950s, although its reputation was tarnished after several fatal accidents and it was grounded in 1954. Extensive research and testing revealed that most of the crashes occurred due to structural failure of the fuselage, resulting from severe stress concentrations at the corners of the square windows that were a feature of the early Comet 1s. After numerous design changes including the now ubiquitous oval-shaped windows, the larger Comet 4 finally flew again in 1958. It then remained in service as a successful airliner into the early 1970s.

By 1951 Whittle was essentially separated from Dorothy, and went from living in a large house in Harrow to a flat in London. He had told his younger son, Ian, that living on his own 'was more conducive to thinking'. At around this time Ian was also showing interest in following in his father's footsteps to become a pilot. When he asked Whittle how he should go ahead with this, he was told that he 'should go to the recruiting office'. Ian did eventually follow this advice, and ended up joining the RAF, where he learned to fly fighters. After leaving the RAF, Ian became a commercial airline pilot, initially with Kuwait Airways, becoming a captain in 1962. In 1970 he joined Cathay Pacific Airways, for whom he flew a range of commercial aircraft, including the Lockheed Tristar, Boeing 707 and finally the Boeing 747. David, Frank's elder son, attended St Andrew's University but led a very reclusive life, not spending much time with the rest of his family. Whittle found this quite difficult to deal with, and he was not nearly as close to David as he was with his younger son.

Early in 1952, Whittle received a brief letter from Lord de L'Isle and Dudley (usually just known as Lord de L'Isle), who was at that time the Secretary of State for Air in the Air Ministry. De L'Isle had fought in the war with the Grenadier Guards, and was awarded a Victoria Cross, the highest award for bravery in the British armed forces. As a young man he graduated from Eton and then Cambridge, as did so many young men with his background, but he did not have a technical education. He had, however, just heard Whittle give a presentation on the development of his original jet engine, and asked if he would expand on his thoughts about future engine designs.

In his letter, De L'Isle asked about the relative benefits of centrifugal and axial compressors, and whether the new bypass engine design was a worthwhile advance. Whittle's reply was rather brief, and he made the point that he no longer had any technical support staff, and was just provided with one secretary! His letter was interesting, however, in that he strongly favoured the centrifugal (or radial) compressor, which he had always used in his designs, suggesting that it 'had been a mistake to go over almost entirely to axial-flow compressors, and to discontinue development of the centrifugal compressor'. He went on to say that he believed the development of the ducted fan was a much more satisfactory design than the turboprop engine that was also being developed.[71] The turboprop consisted of a gas turbine engine that was used to drive a conventional propeller. History has shown that his thoughts about the ducted fan engine were absolutely correct, and almost all large engines are now of this type. His feelings about compressor design, however, have proven to be less prophetic, as the higher efficiency of axial-flow compressors has resulted in them being used almost exclusively in modern jet engines.

By this time Whittle had become a well-known public figure, and his opinions were often sought by the press. However, his forthright, and often controversial, views on a number of important issues of the day unrelated to the airline industry were often not well received by the BOAC chairman, Sir Miles Thomas. Whittle had been appointed chairman of a body known as the Migration Council, which had been lobbying for widespread emigration from the UK to Commonwealth countries. This was most likely at the urging of his long-time friend and original business partner in Power Jets, Sir Rolf Dudley-Williams, who, after leaving the company when it was nationalised, decided to enter the political arena. In a diary note Whittle indicated that he had 'agreed with reluctance to become Chairman of the Migration Council'. At this time Dudley-Williams had been elected as a Conservative Member of Parliament, and had been knighted. He was on the far right of the party, and one of his interests was the controversial plan to encourage recent immigrants to Britain from predominantly non-white countries to return to their 'home countries'. This radical idea had unfortunately gathered some support after the war. During his political career Dudley-Williams had enlisted Whittle from time to time to speak at election rallies in support of his election as he knew that Whittle's fame would help to draw a good crowd.

In mid-1951 Mr Frank Beswick (later to become Lord Beswick), a Labour MP and the Parliamentary Secretary to the Minister of Civil Aviation, who had himself been an RAF pilot during the war, wrote to Sir Miles, indicating that Whittle had been speaking about the role of 'repatriation' of recent UK immigrants during a trip he had made to South Africa. The letter indicated that 'these views are certainly not shared by His Majesty's government and their expression by an official emissary of BOAC is likely to cause embarrassment to His Majesty's Ministers and to prejudice the success of his own mission'. The official letter then ended with the statement, 'Should you propose to send him overseas again I suggest that you should make this clear to him.'[72]

There is little doubt that this letter from a senior government official expedited the termination of Whittle's advisory role at BOAC. He met Sir Miles Thomas and said that he was in an awkward position as he had just bought a house in Harrow to be close to the BOAC office. He told Sir Miles that he was also concerned about losing his office facilities, and the secretarial support that BOAC had provided. There followed a rather formal and testy exchange of letters between Sir Miles and Whittle, ultimately leading to Whittle leaving his informal position as advisor at the end of July 1952. Whittle believed that Sir Miles had impugned his character and in his final letter to the chairman he indicated that he would be seeking 'legal advice', although nothing seemed to come of this.

Just before his departure from BOAC, Whittle had also been hurt by a rather salacious article in *The People* newspaper that clearly gave the impression that, despite his good fortune and prosperous lifestyle, his elderly parents were living in near poverty. On 29 June 1952, the newspaper ran a photo of Whittle, with the headline 'Don't envy Sir Frank his £100,000'. The article went on in a rather condescending manner, with the opening paragraph stating that,

'If you felt a pang of envy when Sir Frank Whittle was awarded £100,000 by the government, this report will cure you. For it reveals how quickly a fortune can melt away and how wagging tongues plague a great and generous man. The gossips have even blamed him for the plight of his parents, though in every way he has been a generous son.' The article then went on to describe how Whittle's father, Moses, was working as a doorman at an ex-serviceman's club for less than £2 per week, and living with his wife in 'two rooms above a cobbler's shop'.

Although Whittle had provided small sums to his parents over the years, he was not very close to them and probably didn't realise that they were struggling to maintain a reasonable lifestyle. He was, naturally, very hurt by the newspaper article, and did subsequently buy a small bungalow for them in Coventry. He also arranged for the bungalow to be passed on to his brother, Arthur, upon the death of both his parents, in part due to the fact that Arthur and his wife had taken on the main role of caring for them.

Whittle had been very loyal to his key supporters and employees over the years, and kept in touch with the core team from the early days of Power Jets. This was somewhat of a 'mutual admiration society', as most of his early team were very strong supporters and in awe of his brilliant mind and unrelenting dedication to bringing his new engine to life. He was particularly fond of Mary Phillips, the secretary who had been completely devoted to him during the start-up of the company. After leaving Power Jets at its dissolution, she had fallen into ill health and was unable to work. When he received his inventors award, Whittle made sure that Ms Phillips shared in his success, if only in a relatively minor way. He arranged to provide her with an annual stipend of £216 per year as, just like all the former Power Jets employees, she had no company pension. In a letter to his solicitor in 1968 he indicated that he would like to modify his original gift to her by increasing it to £300 per year (approximately equal to £5,000 today) until she reached the age of 65, at which point it would increase by a further £100 per year 'in order to account for the inevitable inflation', as Whittle put it in his letter.

Two years after his departure from his informal role at BOAC, Whittle would again become the subject of severe criticism from Sir Miles Thomas. A week after the second BOAC Comet crash in 1954, the popular British weekend magazine the *Picture Post* ran an article by Whittle, entitled 'Why do Comets Crash?' The article was subtitled with 'Sabotage seems the most likely cause of all ... but if not ...'. When asked by the reporter if the age of the aeroplane may have been a factor, Whittle said, 'Yes – it could imply failure through fatigue. That, too, might well be due to repeatedly hitting gusts of air at high speeds.' He went on to say, 'Fatigue-failure through turbulence would occur in the airframe – not in the engines. But I consider this possibility most unlikely.' When asked if he would recommend any changes to the Comet design to make jet-powered flight safer, Whittle made several suggestions. These included putting metal shielding around the jet engines, which in the Comet were imbedded in the wing, and the inclusion of a control system to eliminate any possible engine over-speeding.

Needless to say, the article did not go down well with BOAC and Sir Miles Thomas wrote to Whittle, saying; 'You will not, I am sure, take it amiss when I say that we were shocked by the article that appeared under your signature in 'Picture Post'. The heading was particularly distasteful. Of the recommendations that you made, those which are practical are already in hand.' The letter concluded with typical British understatement, 'We thought, frankly, that the presentation of this article was unhelpful to the Comet cause.'

Subsequent tests showed that some of the crashes were caused by metal fatigue, which was not very far from Whittle's speculation in *Picture Post*.

Although the introduction of the Comet can rightfully be seen as the beginning of the of age of commercial jet travel, the four-year hiatus in Comet production after the crashes enabled other manufacturers, particularly US rival Boeing, to take the leadership in commercial jet aircraft production away from Britain. This continued for several decades until British and French aircraft manufacturers, together with other European partner firms, combined their expertise in the Airbus consortium. These two companies, Boeing and Airbus, one American and one European, now dominate the production of commercial airliners.

The termination of his role as an advisor to BOAC really marked the end of Whittle's close involvement with the aircraft industry. He did comment publicly on aviation matters from time to time, however, particularly when a news item involved the relatively new jet engine. In September 1959, for example, he wrote a letter to the *Daily Telegraph* in response to a BBC report on the problems of noise being produced by the increasing number of jet-propelled aircraft. He noted the report included comments from the chairman of the Noise Abatement Society, to the effect that 'a man who was clever enough to invent the jet aeroplane ought to be clever enough to invent a way of reducing the noise'. Whittle said, 'I don't know if he was getting at me, but it certainly sounded like it.'

Whittle then went on to describe the benefits of the ducted fan or bypass engine that was designed to be more efficient than the straight-through jet engine, and also much quieter. He also said that his first patent for this type of engine was filed in 1936. He went on to conclude that 'my conviction about the merits of the bypass engine remains unshaken, and I venture to predict that it will predominate both for subsonic and supersonic aircraft'.[73] As in so many other things related to jet propulsion, Whittle was absolutely correct in his prediction.

At this stage Whittle was only in his early fifties, and believed that he still had the ability to make a major contribution to the modern practice of engineering. In addition, his personality was not one that would allow him to enjoy a quiet life of retirement, even though his new financial position would have made this an easy choice. He began to think of other ways in which he might keep busy and make use of his considerable engineering talents. He had also kept in touch with a number of organisations and key people who had helped him during his quest to make the jet engine a practical reality. One of these was the Shell Oil Company, which had used their extensive practical knowledge of combustion systems to help him solve the very difficult combustion problems that had held up early development of Whittle's revolutionary new engine. It was Isaac Lubbock who had introduced Whittle to the simple atomising spray combustion system that provided the very high-intensity of combustion that the new engine needed. Lubbock was also a Cambridge engineering graduate, and Whittle had kept in touch over the years of perfecting his revolutionary new engine. During one of their visits together, in which Lubbock would outline some of the new research activities at Shell, he happened to mention the new difficulties being encountered while drilling ever-deeper exploratory oil wells.

Traditional well drilling relies on a long 'string' of drill rods or lengths of pipe down a well hole that connect the drill bit at the bottom of the well with the mechanical drive at the top, which has to turn the complete drill string. In the ever-expanding search for new sources of oil, the wells would continue to get deeper and deeper. As the drill string got longer, the twisting of the drill rods became so extreme that breakages and failures were more and more frequent. This was the type of complex problem that Whittle loved, and it did not take him too long to suggest that a way of drilling very deep wells might be to have a miniature turbine at the bottom of the hole that would turn the drill bit directly. This type of 'down hole' drilling would eliminate the need to rotate the long and fragile mechanical drill string from the top of the well, which was causing so many problems in deep-drilling locations. Whittle's concept was to have a very small high-speed hydraulic turbine at the bottom of the well driving the drill bit directly through reduction gearing. The turbine would be driven by a steady flow of 'drilling mud' that is conventionally used in deep well drilling to cool the drill bit and bring drilling debris to the surface. All that would be needed would then be a down hole piping system, similar to that used for a conventional drill string, in order to provide a steady supply of mud to drive the miniature turbine at the bottom of the drill hole. The concept of turbo-drilling was not, in fact, new and Whittle soon learned that work on this concept had been done in both Germany and Russia, and to a limited extent in the US. The technology was not yet widespread in the industry, however, and he believed that he should be able to improve on the performance of the Russian machines that appeared to be the most advanced to date.

After hearing about Whittle's ideas for changing the way deep well drilling in the West might be achieved, Shell enthusiastically embraced the idea and employed him to work with their drilling engineers to develop this new technique. In late 1953 he was given an employment contract to work for Shell with an annual salary of £3,800, equivalent to approximately £130,000 in today's terms. As part of his contract, Whittle also asked that his secretary, Margaret Lawrence, should be able to accompany him 'as he so desires'. Her address, near where her family lived, was listed as 'Copplestone Farm, Dunsford, near Exeter'. Whittle provided his mailing address in 1954 as 'Flat 2, Culver, Longdown, near Exeter', just 4 miles away from Dunsford. He immediately began designing a very compact turbine unit with a diameter suitable for use in a conventional drill pipe and designed to be powered with a steady flow of drilling mud. This resulted in a US patent, 'High-Speed Turbo-Drill with Reduction Gearing', which was filed in 1956 and finally issued in 1960.[74] The challenges involved in designing such a compact device with enough power to drill through hard ground deep underwater were great, and it was taking much longer than either Whittle or his collaborators within Shell had at first expected. Some two years after Whittle started working on the project the Shell group still seemed to be very positive about the prospects of success, and his salary was increased to the equivalent of £175,000 in today's terms, a sum that included a pension contribution.

As it turned out, a number of practical difficulties made the development of this system much more complex than either Shell or Whittle originally envisaged, and he ended up spending four years, from 1953 to 1957, working full-time on the down hole drilling project. Shell was (and is, of course) a major petroleum producing company, but was not used to developing its own technology for oil well drilling. After spending so much time working with Whittle, and without a practical drill system in sight, Shell management were beginning to lose interest in the project. At the same time, Whittle was again beginning to feel the effects of overwork, and in April 1957 he wrote to Shell indicating that he would like to terminate his contract at the end of October of that year. He indicated in his letter that his resignation was 'in part due to a recurrence of nervous strain'. As a result, they decided to end the development work, and assigned the rights to the technology, and the patents that had been filed, back to Whittle.

At around the same time, and somewhat fortuitously, Whittle had reconnected with two very senior people at Bristol Siddeley Engines (BSE). This firm had recently been established through a merger of the aero engine businesses of Bristol Aero Engines and Armstrong Siddeley Motors as one of the two largest companies (the other being Rolls-Royce) who were then designing and building jet engines in Britain. They were Sir Arnold Hall, with whom Whittle had studied engineering at Cambridge University, and who was now chairman and managing director of BSE, and Stanley Hooker, the brilliant mathematician who had left Rolls-Royce to join BSE as chief engineer. Whittle knew Hooker well, of course, from his groundbreaking work in the early days helping Rolls-Royce get into the jet engine business. Hooker would eventually become famous as the man who was enticed out of retirement in 1971 to lead the company out of bankruptcy, which had been precipitated by development problems with the ground-breaking RB211 turbofan engine. In late 1959 Whittle wrote to Hooker, suggesting that he would like to meet him to discuss his work on the turbo-drill, and to see if BSE might be interested in continuing the development of this new drilling technology.

Both Hall and Hooker had enormous respect for Whittle, and were intrigued to learn of his work with Shell on the drill. They believed that they could perhaps step in to help him with this potentially ground-breaking new technology. In a brief note after meeting with Hooker in mid-October 1959, Whittle commented that Hooker had said that 'he wasn't going to be responsible for turning down one of Whittle's ideas'.[75] The outcome was the formation of a joint venture company, called Bristol-Siddeley Whittle Tools, or BSWT, for the main purpose of commercialising Whittle's innovative new 'turbo drill', as it was now being called. The new company continued development work, and a working prototype was used in several drilling trials. There were, however, many problems in servicing such a complex device located at the bottom of a deep well working in very harsh conditions. As a result, take-up of the new concept was slow, and it did not succeed in displacing the more conventional simple drilling technique in which the drill string was powered at the top of the well. An approach was also made to the Hughes Tool company in the US, but after some trials they decided not to take over development of the turbo-drill.

Meanwhile, in late November 1959 Whittle was a passenger on Trans World Airlines' (TWA) inaugural flight of the new Boeing

707, the new jetliner that would become the long-serving workhorse for most major international airlines at the time. He was finally beginning to take some 'personal time', and in December 1960 he sailed to Australia and New Zealand on the maiden voyage of the *Oriana*. This was the new flagship passenger liner of the Orient Steam Navigation Company, later to become the Peninsular and Oriental Steam Navigation Company (or P&O). Whittle had embarked on what was to be a world tour, but after nearly two months he disembarked in Naples and flew back to England. This may have been due to ill health, or more likely as someone not used to long periods of leisure activity he probably just became bored of the luxurious, but somewhat constricted, life aboard ship.

Detailed development work on the turbo-drill concept continued on until 1965, but no customers within the rather conservative oil industry could be found. The widespread introduction of this new innovation was greatly hampered by the takeover of BSE by Rolls-Royce in 1968. Support for BSWT and the turbo-drill concept dried up within the new merged company, as they focused on developing the next generation of large jet engines.

Whittle tried desperately to see if he could interest the government in providing support for continued development of the turbo-drill. In a letter to the Ministry of Technology he said that he was 'playing his last card' by offering a substantial portion of his own shareholding to the government. However, no government funding was forthcoming, and the final blow to the company was the infamous bankruptcy of Rolls-Royce on 4 February 1971, resulting from overspending on development of the RB211, the first of a new generation of large jet engines. The bad news for Whittle came in a letter from Stanley Hooker, who had been brought out of retirement to lead the efforts to restructure the company as the new nationalised entity Rolls-Royce 1971 Ltd. Hooker told Whittle that the new company had been given a strict remit to work on 'aero engines and defence projects only', and it was therefore not possible to provide any support for development of the turbo-drill. Hooker also noted that the new company even had to give up their interests in motor cars and large diesel engines.[76]

BSWT was formally wound up in 1972, after Whittle wrote a letter to the remaining shareholders in which he said, 'I wish to relinquish all possible financial benefit from the turbo-drill and to make available for you and any additional individuals you may recruit the patents and drawings which I now own.'[77] Unfortunately, no other shareholders came forward to take over the challenging development project. This finally ended all work on the turbo-drill, although a somewhat similar down hole rotary 'mud motor' began to be used for deep well drilling. Somewhat ironically, this had been proposed in the 1930s by René Moineau, a French aviation pioneer. It was, however, a positive displacement type of device, which turned out to be much more suitable for deep well drilling. These are now used widely for the type of directional drilling operations needed for natural gas 'fracking' operations.

For some time Whittle had been living near the small village of Dunsford, on the edge of Dartmoor national park, with Margaret Lawrence, his former secretary at BOAC and frequent social companion. Dunsford was a quiet country village that seemed to suit Whittle, and was close to Exeter in Devon where some of Margaret's extended family lived. In 1962 he bought a house not too far away near the village of Chagford in the Dartmoor National park. Walland Hill is a large house with a number of outbuildings set in about 8 acres of land with good views over the rolling countryside (see Plate 19). He shared the house with Margaret, who took on the role of housekeeper in addition to her duties as Whittle's secretary. This was to remain Whittle's main home for some thirteen years until his move to the US in 1976.

In late 1966 Whittle again visited the US, and this time he visited the Aerospace Research Laboratory at Wright-Patterson Air Force

Base in Dayton, Ohio. This was a memorable visit, as the chief scientist at that time was Hans von O'Hain, who had developed his version of the jet engine in Germany during the Second World War.

O'Hain had emigrated to the US after the war and was now one of the key people working on jet engine development in the US. At this time, more than twenty years after the end of the war, the correspondence between O'Hain and Whittle was very friendly. Whittle had spent some of the time at O'Hain's nearby house, and clearly both men had enjoyed the opportunity to compare their work on developing the very first operational jet engines in their respective home countries during the war. In his letter thanking Whittle for his visit, O'Hain said, 'We shall always remember with pleasure the interesting hours we spent together during this, your first visit to the Aerospace Research Laboratories.' O'Hain then finished his letter by suggesting that Whittle might like to make a longer visit to the Wright-Patterson Base in order to work on areas of research that would be of mutual interest.[78]

From 1966 to early 1967 Whittle was asked by Rolls-Royce to help them fight a patent infringement case brought by a French engine manufacturer, Societé Rateau. Unbeknownst to Rolls-Royce, or Whittle, this company had applied for, and received, patents for a jet engine very similar to Whittle's original design. These patents were applied for in 1939 in France, and also in 1941 in the UK. However, because of wartime restrictions, the complete specifications were not available until 1951.[79] Rateau eventually brought a case of patent infringement to the UK courts in 1966. Rolls-Royce had notice of the upcoming case for some time and had been actively working to make a case that the patents filed by Rateau were insufficient to overturn any of Whittle's original patents, or the ones subsequently filed by Rolls-Royce. In order to strengthen their case they asked Whittle to work with them and to appear in the UK court as an expert witness.

Although he was initially very confident that he would be able to demolish the claims made by Rateau, once he was briefed on the legal complexities of the case Whittle became somewhat more reluctant to appear in court. In the end, however, he agreed to take the stand on behalf of Rolls-Royce in what would become the longest and most expensive patent lawsuit in the UK up to that time. The case finally came to court at the beginning of November 1966, and lasted until early February 1967. Whittle was just one of many witnesses for the defendants, but he was, of course, well known and his straightforward evidence clearly carried great weight with the judge. In the end, the case for patent infringement against Rolls-Royce was lost as the judge ruled that the Rateau patents were simply invalid in light of Whittle's original patent and subsequent patents held by Rolls-Royce.

Whittle once again became engaged in helping Rolls-Royce fight a patent battle in late 1968, related to their new RB211 engine design. This new engine design was ground-breaking at the time, and took the concept of the now ubiquitous 'two-spool' turbojet engine one step further by adding a third spool designed to power only the large fan section at the front of the engine. This is still the basic engine architecture used by Rolls-Royce in its current crop of large jet engines, the Trent. The added complexity of this design enabled each 'spool' in the engine to run more closely at optimum speed for the size of the blading being used. The Rolls-Royce assistant patent manager wrote to Whittle in September 1968, asking for his help with the patent application in order to convince the patent office that the new three-spool design was 'novel' enough to secure a patent. Whittle replied five days later, and in characteristic style he pointed out two weak points in the patent application. He once again acted as an expert witness for Rolls-Royce, enabling them to successfully obtain the patent. This basic design is still the only large three-spool engine being manufactured for commercial aircraft.

During this period Whittle had remained in touch with Mr Laidlaw of Laidlaw Drew and Co., who had helped him with the original combustion problems. Laidlaw had for a long time owned a holiday property in Jamaica, and often invited Whittle to join him there. During one of these visits Whittle purchased a large property in the Spring Farm Rose Hall area of Montego Bay. He named the house Ladywood Villa, as a reminder of the many years he spent working on his radical new engine design at the Ladywood Works in Lutterworth. The property included a four-bedroom bungalow located close to the beach as well as a separate cottage with two additional bedrooms. In order to cover some of the expenses, he arranged to rent the house out to holidaymakers when he was not there, and employed a housekeeper to look after the guests and oversee the house in his absence. However, Whittle spent much less time at the Jamaican property than he had originally thought he might. This was mostly due to the fact that he really was not the type to spend much time relaxing on vacation while there was work to do on some new project. As a result, and with the costs of maintaining the property escalating, he sold the house in 1974 to the current owners. It is still known as Ladywood Villa, and is listed as a holiday rental property by the Russel family, who purchased it from Whittle.

By the beginning of 1976, Whittle's work on the turbo-drill had come to an end, and being somewhat unsettled, he began to think about his future. He had continued to maintain contact with Hazel 'Tommie' Steenberg (née Hall), the American nurse and fellow patient he had first met during his long stay in the Bethesda Naval Hospital in 1947. They had corresponded over nearly thirty years and Tommie often accompanied Whittle during his frequent travels in the US. As a result, and to the surprise of his sons and estranged wife, he decided to move to the US and marry Tommie. This undoubtedly also came as a shock to Margaret Lawrence, with whom he had shared the large house in Chagford for nearly fifteen years. As a result, and likely with a somewhat guilty conscience, Whittle signed over the house to Ms Lawrence when he left to marry Tommie and live permanently in the US.

Although he had initiated proceedings to divorce his wife, Dorothy, Whittle was somewhat taken aback to realise that it was not final when he married Tommie on 5 November 1976. As a result, once the divorce from Dorothy was finalised he arranged a very quiet second marriage ceremony on 26 January 1977. After their marriage, Whittle and Tommie lived in Columbia, Maryland, just outside Washington DC, until Whittle's death in 1996. Their town house, on Wilde Lake Terrace overlooking a small lake, was only about 25 miles from the Bethesda military hospital (now known as the Walter Reed National Military Medical Center) where they had first met nearly thirty years before they were married. Although he would make frequent visits back to the UK, Whittle now spent most of his time in the US, where he continued to write and lecture on the origins of the jet engine from time to time.

Whittle's new home in Maryland was about a half-hour drive away from the US Naval Academy in Annapolis. He had previous contacts with researchers at there, and as a result he was appointed to a part-time role as the NAVAIR research professor in 1977. NAVAIR is the widely used abbreviation in the US Navy for Naval Air Systems Command, the air-wing of the US Navy. He continued working in that role for several years, and in 1981 published a text book entitled *Gas Turbine Aero-Thermodynamics*,[80] based in part on his lectures there. He also continued to give special lectures and seminars from time to time both in the UK and the US. A Naval Academy aerospace engineering professor was quoted as saying, 'Whittle's name deserves to be placed alongside Einstein's and Newton's because he was very much instrumental in revolutionizing aviation.'[81]

Whittle continued to visit the UK from time to time, usually to either make a presentation or take part in a celebration of the birth of the jet engine. During these trips he was often a passenger on Concorde, the world's first successful supersonic airliner. This was also very convenient for him, as Columbia, Maryland, is close to Washington DC and only about an hour's drive from Washington Dulles airport, from where the British Airways aircraft flew to London Heathrow. The first scheduled flight of Concorde to the US was to Dulles in May 1976. Supersonic travel was only made possible, of course, because of his pioneering work on the jet engine, and this was a great source of pride for him.

Whittle was very pleased to be awarded the Order of Merit (OM) by Queen Elizabeth II in 1986. This is one of the most prestigious of the many honours that may be awarded in the UK. Rather than being recommended by the government of the day, or by an awards committee, as is the case for most British awards, the OM is awarded as the personal gift of the Sovereign. The OM is also limited to only twenty-four living honourees, making it one of the most exclusive honours to be awarded by the Crown. In some rare cases the OM has also been awarded to non-British recipients in an 'honorary' capacity. At the time of writing, the earliest living recipient of the OM is Lord Foster of Thames Bank, the celebrated architect, while the most recent is Sir Venkatraman Ramakrishnan, winner of the 2009 Nobel prize in Chemistry. Other notable recipients have included Winston Churchill, Mother Teresa and Nelson Mandela. There are currently only four female recipients of the OM, including Dame Ann Dowling, appointed in 2016. Somewhat fittingly, Professor Dowling's research is related to aircraft acoustics, and she served as Head of the Department of Engineering at Cambridge University from 2009 until 2014. She also served as President of the Royal Academy of Engineering from 2014 to 2019, the academy's first female in the role.

An important long-term partnership with Whittle came to an end on 9 October 1987, with the death of Sir Rolf Dudley-Wiliams, who had been a friend since their days as RAF cadets and a key employee of Power Jets from the very beginning. He had been the main commercial driver of Power Jets, particularly in the early days, which enabled Whittle to focus almost entirely on the technical aspects of jet engine development. Dudley-Williams had been a Conservative MP from 1951 to 1966, serving as the parliamentary private secretary to the Secretary of State for War in 1958, and then to the Minister of Agriculture from 1960 to 1964. He was quoted as saying 'I went into politics because I was so annoyed with Stafford Cripps that I wanted to wipe the floor with him.' Cripps, of course, had been a Labour MP and Minister of Aircraft Production during the war, and had overseen the nationalisation of Power Jets in 1944.

Whittle had been a smoker from his very early days in the RAF, as were many serving officers, and on 9 August 1996, he died in the US of complications due to lung cancer at the age of 89. His ashes were taken back to the UK, where they are now interred at the RAF College in Cranwell. In his will Whittle left his house, Walland Hill in Chagford, together with 'all personal chattels therein', to Margaret Lawrence, his long-time companion. He left the balance of his estate to be divided among his two sons, David and Ian, his wife, Lady Hazel Whittle, as well as his brother, Albert, his sister Catherine and his nieces and nephews. Sir Frank Whittle has been honoured in many ways both by the RAF and other institutions. He was the recipient of many awards, as listed below:

- Member of the Order of Merit
- Knight Commander of the Order of the British Empire
- Companion of the Order of the Bath
- Commander of the Legion of Merit (United States)
- Rumford Medal
- Louis E. Levy Medal
- Honorary Fellow of the Royal Aeronautical Society

- Charles Stark Draper Prize
- Prince Philip Medal
- Louis E. Levy Medal
- Fellow of the Royal Society
- Honorary Fellow of the Royal Aeronautical Societ
- Daniel Guggenheim Medal

A memorial service to honour Whittle was held on 16 November 1996 in Westminster Abbey. The Dean of Westminster officiated and the Queen was represented by Sir George Edwards, FRS, and the Duke of Edinburgh was represented by Sir David Davies, FRS. Lord Kings Norton read the first lesson, while the Duke of Kent read the second lesson. Ian Whittle, Sir Frank's son, paid tribute to his father, and Sir Michael Graydon, Chief of the Air Staff, also gave an address. After the service there was a fly past by RAF Tornados and two Meteors, which were the first British jet fighters, and the only Allied jet aircraft to take part in the Second World War.

To mark the seventieth anniversary of the first flight powered by Whittle's revolutionary new engine, a ceremony was held at RAF Cranwell on 15 May 2011. A highlight was the unveiling of a fibreglass replica of the original Gloster E.28/39 aircraft that first flew on 15 May 1941. This replica is now on display in the Jet Age Museum in Gloucester.

Whittle's genius and contributions to the nation were honoured in a much more public way when a memorial stone dedicated to his memory was unveiled in Westminster Abbey in London, on 12 April 2000. The stone is inscribed with 'Frank Whittle Inventor & Pioneer of the Jet Engine, 1907–1996'. This is located in the Royal Air Force Chapel in the Abbey, which also contains the graves of two other prominent RAF members, Lord Dowding and Lord Trenchard. Whittle would no doubt be incredibly proud that his accomplishments are honoured alongside these two prominent members of the service that he loved.

A number of other memorials to Whittle have been erected across England, but particularly in those areas where he conducted most of his work on the new engine. These include the 'Whittle Arches' in Coventry, where a statue of Whittle in full RAF uniform by Faith Winter is displayed under two large stainless steel arches outside Coventry Transport Museum. This was unveiled by Whittle's son, Ian, during a televised event on 1 June 2007, and is shown in Plate 20.

In Lutterworth, where much of the early work on the new jet engine was done by Whittle and his colleagues, a wonderful replica of the E.28/39 is on display centred in a roundabout marking the main road to the original factory. This original piece, shown in Plate 21, gives a wonderful impression of the first little jet climbing into the sky just after take-off. There is also a bust of Whittle in the town of Lutterworth, and many other plaques and monuments around the country that commemorate the ground-breaking accomplishments of this gifted engineer who dedicated most of his working life to bringing his invention to fruition.

His name has even been used to name a school in Coventry. This was originally called Frank Whittle Primary, but was later renamed as the Sir Frank Whittle Primary School. The school even has a replica jet engine donated by Whittle in its reception area. Also in Coventry there is the Midland Air Museum next to Coventry Airport, which contains the Sir Frank Whittle Jet Heritage Centre.

There are many other acknowledgements of Whittle's contributions in the industrial heartland of England, but he has also been recognised further afield. In Cambridge, where Whittle received the advanced engineering education that helped to advance his ideas, there is the Whittle Laboratory, attached to the Engineering Department. This specialised facility is dedicated to research on jet engine components. Also in Cambridge, Peterhouse College, where

Whittle studied as an undergraduate, has a new building just known as the Whittle Building, which was opened in 2015.

Not surprisingly, Rolls-Royce has several reminders of the contributions that Whittle made to their endeavours in designing and building jet engines. These include Whittle House, the main office complex in Bristol, while in Derby there are two roads, Sir Frank Whittle Road and Sir Frank Whittle Way.

Also, in a different type of recognition, the UK-based Institution of Mechanical Engineers awards the Sir Frank Whittle Medal annually to an engineer 'for outstanding and sustained achievement which has contributed to the well-being of the nation'.

Postscript

The development of the jet engine was one of the most significant milestones in the twentieth century, and has enabled many millions of people to travel around the globe every year. The ready availability of intercontinental air travel, made possible by the modern jet engine, has resulted in unprecedented mobility for millions of people who otherwise would never have left their home countries. In fact, according to the International Air Transport Association (IATA), more than 3.5 billion passengers took to the air in 2016. The engines supplied by the three major manufacturers, Rolls-Royce, GE and Pratt & Whitney, can all be traced back to Whittle's original patent and his successful development of the WU (Whittle Unit) engine that first ran in 1937. These companies are all now multi-billion dollar businesses, employing tens of thousands of people. Most large civil jet engines today are actually turbofan engines, in which a large fan at the front of the engine, driven by one section of the turbine, provides a very large flow of air that bypasses the main core of the engine. This concept was actually first envisaged by Whittle, who filed a patent for the concept in 1936. However, the patent expired before the concept became widely adopted for civil airliners late in the twentieth century.

It should be noted that jet engines were also developed in the early years of the Second World War by Hans O'Hain, in Germany. O'Hain, unlike Whittle, came from a middle-class family, and had received a PhD degree in Physics from the University of Gottingen, one of the best technical universities in Germany. His engine design used an axial-flow compressor rather than the centrifugal design used by Whittle. O'Hain also had independent means and was able to use private funds to develop his early engine design much faster than did Whittle. It also seems quite likely that he had seen Whittle's first jet engine patent, which had been filed in January 1930. As a student he owned and drove a sports car, which he would regularly take for servicing to a nearby garage. During one of these visits he described his concept for a novel engine to the garage owner, who agreed to build a working model of the engine. O'Hain was ultimately successful in developing an engine that powered the world's very first jet flight in a Heinkel He 178 in August 1939, some twenty-one months before the first flight of Whittle's engine in the Gloster E.28/39. After the war, and especially when they both emigrated to the US, Whittle and O'Hain became quite close friends and enjoyed reminiscing about the early struggles to get the jet engine accepted as the successor to piston engines.

It is clear that Frank Whittle was not only a technical genius, but had the drive and self-confidence in his own abilities that enabled him to pursue his dream to a successful conclusion. The development of the jet engine came to the fore during a major war, which meant that it was likely developed into a commercial product sooner than it would have been during peacetime. However, the fact that it was developed by a serving RAF officer with significant government backing also meant that Whittle lost the opportunity for major financial reward. This was quite unlike the early development of the automobile, for example, which resulted in family fortunes being created by pioneers such as Henry Ford, Karl Benz, Walter Chrysler and Louis Chevrolet.

The development of the jet engine can also be seen to mark the transition of engineering from a largely 'craft-based' endeavour to a 'science-based' profession. Whittle was able to use the very strong mathematical and analytical skills that he had learned while studying engineering at Cambridge University to analyse the performance of his new propulsion concept. These are the kinds of skills that are now taught to all professional engineering students in every discipline, and provide the basis for developing much of the 'new technology' that continues to transform society in the same way that Whittle's jet engine transformed long-distance transportation. It is also interesting to see that there is still a strong connection between Whittle's engineering legacy and Cambridge University. Churchill College, a Cambridge college that attracts a large number of engineering students, holds Whittle's original papers in its archives, together with those of Sir Winston Churchill and many other prominent people primarily associated with Churchill and the Second World War.

Whittle's first wife, Dorothy, died in Surrey in 1996 at the age of 92, while Margaret Lawrence, who had been his housekeeper and companion for so many years and never married, died in 2000. She bequeathed Walland Hill, the Chagford house she had shared with Whittle, to two of her relatives, Ann Lawrence and Richard Wheeler. Whittle's second wife, Tommie, continued to live in their apartment in Maryland until her death in 2007. His eldest son, David, who had been estranged from his father for many years, died in 2013, and his youngest son, Ian, continues to give talks about his father's work from time to time.

There is no doubt that the invention and early development of the jet engine was one of the most significant engineering accomplishments of the twentieth century. The contributions of Sir Frank Whittle in conceiving his original engine design, and then his persistent determination to build and test a successful prototype, has provided many millions of people with the ability to travel to almost any part of the world in a matter of hours. That he was able to accomplish this, often in the face of seemingly insurmountable odds, is a tribute to one of the towering minds of the twentieth century.

Appendix 1

Flight Magazine, 11 October 1945

Early History of the Whittle Jet Propulsion Gas Turbine

By Air Commodore Frank Whittle, CBE, RAF, MA, Hon MIMechE

There have been many attempts to solve the gas turbine problem in the past. The records in the Patent Office would probably show that the problem of the gas turbine has engaged the attention of inventors almost to the same extent as perpetual motion. It will suffice to say that the constant-pressure gas turbine is an old idea, and that there have been many attempts to produce a practicable engine of this sort, but at the time I started thinking on the subject, i.e. in 1928, the many failures had led to a general belief in the engineering world that it had no future.

The main argument against the gas turbine was that the maximum temperatures permissible with materials available, or likely to be available, was such that the ratio of positive to negative work in the constant-pressure cycle could not be great enough to allow a reasonable margin of useful work to be obtained, allowing for the losses in the turbine and compressor. There seemed to be a curious tendency to take it for granted that the low efficiencies of turbine and compressors commonly cited were inevitable. I did not share the prevalent pessimism because I was convinced that big improvements in these efficiencies were possible, and, in the application of jet propulsion aircraft, I realised that there were certain favourable factors not present in other applications, namely:

i) The fact that the low temperature at high altitudes made possible a greater ratio of positive to negative work for a given maximum cycle temperature.
ii) A certain proportion of the compression could be obtained at high efficiency by the ram effect of forward speed, thereby raising the average efficiency of the whole compression process.
iii) The expansion taking place in the turbine element of such an engine was only that which was necessary to drive the compressor: and therefore only part of the expansion process was subject to turbine losses.

I first started thinking about this general subject in 1928, in my fourth term as a flight cadet at the RAF College, Cranwell. Each term we had to write a science thesis, and in my fourth term as a flight cadet at the RAF College, Cranwell.

Appendix 2

List of Patents Held by Whittle

Application Date	Application No.	Title
1930/01/16	347 206	Propulsion of Aircraft
1930/10/16	347 766	Centrifugal Compressors
1931/07/23	375 104	Supercharging Aircraft Engines
1935/05/16	456 976	Centrifugal Compressors
1935/05/18	456 980	Propulsion of Aircraft
1935/05/19	457 972	Electrical Transmission of Power
1935/07/25	461 887	I/C Turbines
1936/03/04	471 368	Propulsion of Aircraft
1937/12/15	511 278	Turbines and Compressors
1938/02/25	512 064	Propulsion of Aircraft
1939/12/09	577 971	Aircraft Propulsion Systems
1939/12/09	577 972	Liquid Fuel Burners and Vaporisers
1939/12/19	583 022	Turbine Cooling
1940/03/02	583 111	Two-tier contra-rotating rotors
1940/03/02	583 112	Fore and aft fans
1940/03/02	584 126	Centrifugal Compressors
1941/12/01	593 403	Propulsion of Aircraft
1942.02/02	582 978	Gas turbine exhausts
1942/04/07	587 511	Compressors

Application Date	Application No.	Title
1942/05/13	587 512	Exhaust Systems – insulation
1942/11/17	588 084	Combustion Engine with Ammonia injection
1943/06/23	615 885	Reduction of Drag and propulsion of Hydrodynamic bodies
1947/07/18	629 143	Aircraft power unit installations
1948/09/01	641 062	Manufacture of metals
1949/03/01	677 835	Rotary Compressors (pre-whirl)
1954/12/10	755 207	Well drilling systems and methods of operation

Notes

1. Golley, J., *Genesis of the Jet*, Airlife Publishing, 1998.
2. www.leamingtonhistory.co.uk/leamington-college-for-boys-slideshow
3. Stodola, A., *Steam Turbines – with an appendix on Gas Turbines – and the future of Heat Engines*, Archibald Constable & Co., 1905.
4. Golley.
5. Obituary, *Daily Telegraph*, 1996.
6. UK Patent #1833 – A Method for Rising Inflammable Air for the Purposes of Producing Motion and Facilitating .
7. UK Patent #347,206, 16 April 1931.
8. Whittle Archives, Churchill College, Cambridge.
9. Golley.
10. Whittle, F., *Jet*, Frederick Muller Ltd, 1953.
11. Churchill College Archives, Cambridge.
12. Churchill College Archives.
13. Bramson, M.L., Report on the Whittle System of Aircraft Propulsion (Theoretical Stage), October 1935.
14. Golley.
15. Golley.
16. Whittle, F., 'The Early History of the Whittle Jet Propulsion Gas Turbine', IMechE 1st James Clayton Lecture, 1945.
17. Whittle, F., *Jet*.
18. Whittle, F., Memo re: FW visit to Air Ministry, 10 May 1940.
19. Whittle, F., Memo on conference at the Air Ministry, 26 March 1940.
20. Golley.
21. Whittle, F. Memo on conference at the Air Ministry, 12 April 1940.
22. Whittle, F., Letter to Sir Henry Tizard, 2 June 1940.

23. Whittle, F., Memo on interview with Lord Beaverbrook, 9 July 1940.
24. Tedder, A.W., Letter to Mr L.L. Whyte of Power Jets, 21 August 1940.
25. Whittle, F., Memo on talk with Mr Tobin, London, 3 September 1940.
26. Whittle, F., Notes on resignation of Mr Whyte, 4 September 1940.
27. Ibid.
28. Whittle, F., Visit to Air Vice-Marshal Tedder, 6 September 1940.
29. Whittle, F., Visit of Air Chief Marshal Sir Wilfred Freeman, 18 October 1940.
30. Whittle, F., *Jet*.
31. Letter from the Director of Contracts for the Ministry of Aircraft Production, 15 November 1940.
32. Memo to file from F. Whittle, 28 January 1941.
33. Golley.
34. Golley.
35. Test Flying Memorial, www.thunder-and-lightnings.co.uk/memorial
36. Whittle, Talks with S.B. Wilks, 19 May 1941.
37. Whittle, Meeting at Rolls-Royce Ltd, Derby, 17 June 1941.
38. Letter to Whyte from F. Whittle, 2 July 1941.
39. Furse, Anthony, *Wilfrid Freeman: the genius behind Allied survival and air supremacy 1939 to 1945*, Staplehurst. Spellmount, 2000.
40. Whittle, F., Memo re: Visit of Mr Hives and Mr Sidgreaves RR, 30 January 1942.
41. Whittle, F., Memo re: Talk with Mr Hives at Derby, 31 January 1942.
42. Whittle, F., Letter to Air Marshal Linnell, 12 April 1942.
43. Linnell, F., Letter to F. Whittle, 19 April 1942.
44. Halford, F., Letter to F. Whittle, 14 May 1942.
45. Golley.
46. Ibid.
47. Whittle, F., Visit to MAP, 19 August 1942.
48. Roxbee Cox, H., Memorandum, 16 September 1942.
49. Power Jets, Visit of Messrs Sidgreaves & Hives (RR), 8 October 1942.
50. Whittle, F., Talk with Mr Hives, Mr Elliot and Dr Roxbee Cox, 12 December 1942.
51. Hooker, S., *Not Much of an Engineer*.

52. F. Whittle, F., Letter to Major Halford, 25 May 25, 1942.
53. Linnell, F., Letter to Power Jets, 19 April 1942.
54. Roxbee Cox, H., Memorandum, 16 September 1942.
55. Power Jets, Visit of Messrs Sidgreaves & Hives (RR), 8 October 1942.
56. Whittle, F., Talk with Mr Hives, Mr Elliot and Dr Roxbee Cox, 12 December 1942.
57. Hooker, S., *Not Much of an Engineer.*
58. Tinling, J.C.B., Letter to H. Roxbee Cox, 7 June 1943.
59. Whittle, F., The Assets of Power Jets, 16 June 1943.
60. Whittle, F., Letter to Sir Stafford Cripps, MAP, 16 June 1943.
61. Whittle, F., Visit of Dr Guy, 1 January 1944.
62. Whittle, F., Interview with the Minister, 3 January 1944.
63. Whittle, F., Phone call to Dr Roxbee Cox, 6 January 1944.
64. Whittle, F., *Jet.*
65. Whittle, F., Party at Buckingham Palace, 1 March 1944.
66. Cripps, Stafford, Letter to F. Whittle, 29 March 1944.
67. Whittle, F., Letter to Stafford Cripps, 3 April 1944.
68. Hooker, S., Letter to F. Whittle, 1 December 1944.
69. Whittle, F., letter to H. Roxbee Cox, 22 January 1946.
70. Hooker, S., Letter to Mr R.C. McLeod, 29 April 1946.
71. Shepherd, J., Report on tour of USA as PA to Air Commodore F. Whittle, C.B.E., 1946.
72. Carla Clavelle, Tommie's daughter, personal reminiscence, 2016.
73. Lord Kings Norton of Wotton Underwood – a biographical sketch, author unknown, 1992.
74. Whittle, F., *Jet.*
75. Whittle, F., Report on Visit of Sir Frank Whittle to Canada and USA, Sept. 16 to Oct. 5, 1948.
76. Whittle, F., Quoted in a Smithsonian Institution Press Release, 8 November 1949.
77. Whittle, F., Letter to Lord de L'Isle and Dudley, 8 February 1952.
78. Letter to Sir Miles Thomas from Frank Beswick, 1951.
79. Whittle, F., 'Reducing Jet Noise', *Daily Telegraph*, 12 September 1959.
80. Whittle, F., US Patent 2,937,008, 1960.
81. Whittle, F., Memo on Visit to BSE, 16 October 1959.

82. Hooker, S., Letter to F. Whittle, 12 April 1972.
83. Whittle, F., Letter to BSWT shareholders, 8 May 1972.
84. O'Hain, H., Letter to F. Whittle, 19 October 1966.
85. Rolls-Royce and the Rateau Patents, Harry Pearson, 1989.
86. Whittle, F., *Gas Turbine Aerothermodynamics*, Pergamon Press, 1981.
87. Saarlas, Prof. Maido, *The Baltimore Sun*, 14 August 1966.

Index

Bolton, Lancashire, 1
Borton, Group Captain Robert, 8
Bramson, M.L., 33–6, 48

Concorde, 171
Coventry, 1–2, 20–1, 78, 158, 174
Cripps, Stafford, 121–2, 125–6, 128–30, 132–3, 150, 172
Cryton, Air Marshal, 138

Dudley-Williams, Rolf, 13, 28, 32–3, 36, 59, 73, 90, 94, 97, 126, 156, 171–2

Earlsdon, 2
E.28/39, 82–6, 88, 97, 114, 116, 121, 150, 173–4, 177
    Replica, 174

Garlick, Sarah, 1
Griffith, A.A., 15–16, 40, 134

Halford, Frank, 107–108, 116, 135, 154
Hall, Hazel 'Tommie', *see* Steenberg, Hazel 'Tommie'

King George VI, 131, 145

Ladywood Villa, 169
Ladywood Works, 44–7, 51, 53, 57, 89, 95, 98, 169
Laidlaw Drew & Co., 41–2, 169
Leamington, 1–8
Linnell, Air Vice Marshal, 102–103, 106–108

Milverton School, 2

O'Hain, Hans, 167, 176–7

Peterhouse, 30–1, 38, 174
Pye, David R., 39, 52–3, 59, 62, 66–7, 81

RAF, 5–6, 9–10, 13–15, 17, 19–20, 22–3, 36–7, 56, 66, 69, 80, 86, 98, 117, 124, 127–8, 131, 133, 137, 143, 146, 155, 172, 174
RAF Cranwell, 5–7, 9–10, 13–15, 20, 28, 84–6, 88, 172–3, 180
Rolls-Royce, vi, 40, 44, 47, 55, 75, 88–9, 95–103, 105, 109, 116–22, 124, 126–7, 132, 134–8, 140, 148, 154, 163–5, 167–8, 175–6

Roxbee Cox, Harold, 71, 78–9, 115–16, 123, 125, 128–31, 134–5, 138, 143, 152

Steenberg, Hazel 'Tommie', 142, 151, 169–70, 172, 178
Straight, Whitney, 146–7, 149, 151–2

Tinling, J.C.B., 32–4, 36, 45, 58–9, 73, 90, 94, 97, 121, 123–6

Walland Hill, 166, 172, 178

Whittle Arches, 174
Whittle, David, 20, 130, 155, 172, 178
Whittle, Lady Dorothy, 20, 23, 147, 149, 154, 170, 178
Whittle Building, Peterhouse, 175
Whittle, Ian, 20, 130, 147, 150, 154–5, 172–4, 178
Whittle, Lady Hazel, *see* Steenberg, Hazel 'Tommie'
Whittle Laboratory, Cambridge, 174
Whittle, Moses, 1–2, 4, 158